C000185152

Coventry

History and Guide

David McGrory

ALAN SUTTON

First published in the United Kingdom in 1993 by
Alan Sutton Publishing Ltd
Phoenix Mill · Far Thrupp · Stroud · Gloucestershire

First published in the United States of America in 1993 by
Alan Sutton Publishing Inc. · 83 Washington Street · Dover · NH 03820

Copyright © David McGrory, 1993

All rights reserved. No part of this publication may be reproduced,
stored in a retrieval system, or transmitted, in any form or by any
means, electronic, mechanical, photocopying, recording or otherwise,
without the prior permission of publishers and copyright holder.

British Library Cataloguing in Publication Data

McGrory, David
    Coventry: History and Guide
    I. Title
    942.498

    ISBN 0-7509-0194-2

Library of Congress Cataloging in Publication Data applied for

Jacket illustration: The ruined shell of the Cathedral Church of St
Michael (*Viewfinder Photo Library*)

For Heather, Dad, Will, Caz and John

Typeset in 10/13 Times.
Typesetting and origination by
Alan Sutton Limited.
Printed in Great Britain by
The Bath Press, Avon.

Contents

CHAPTER ONE

Beginnings

C oventry is a far more ancient place than many assume. It grew in the once huge Forest of Arden, around two hills and a valley of rivers, streams and pools which teemed with fish and game. Prehistoric man passed through the area leaving his flint tools scattered around the city districts. The centre of the city, however, has been so affected by centuries of occupation and development that any evidence of man's early passage or settlement, if it existed, has long been obliterated. It is possible, though, that an early trackway passed through here, and our ancient ancestors may have stopped to fish and hunt in the valley before heading southwards towards Baginton and beyond, where evidence of their passage has often been found.

A trackway through Coventry was certainly known and used by the Romans. This Roman road probably ran from Leicester to Mancetter on the Watling Street in the north, through Hartshill, Harbury, Exhall, Coventry, and south to Baginton, and Wappenbury, and finally joining the Fosse at Chesterton. It is believed that when Boudicca rose against the Romans in AD 61 and nearly succeeded in destroying Roman rule in Britain, her army faced the last legion at Mancetter. Here the Celts were out-manoeuvred and slaughtered in their thousands. Boudicca left the battlefield and took her own life, her body being secretly buried so it would not fall into the hands of the Romans. The aftermath of the battle left the Romans with a large number of untrained horses, which, it is thought, were taken and trained at the Roman army camp at Baginton. During excavations there a huge timber circle known as a *gyrus* was discovered, the only one in Western Europe. Horses were driven around this circle as soldiers stood on the perimeter beating their shields, the sound of which echoed around the *gyrus*, thus conditioning the horses for battle.

Other evidence of the passage of Romans through Coventry has also been discovered. One of the earliest Roman finds in the city was found in the summer of 1792. At a depth of 5–6 ft below Broadgate a pavement was discovered on which was found a bronze coin of the Emperor Nero (AD 54–68), and on 4 January 1793 the *Coventry Mercury* reported that:

Opposite: Remains of the west entrance of Coventry Priory. These remains once saw the feet of a thousand pilgrims. These remains can be seen on Smith's sketch of 1597 (page 16)

An eighteenth-century engraving showing the Foleshill Hoard, found in 1793, which contained 1,800 Roman coins. The illustration is taken from the *Gentleman's Magazine*

On the 17th December last, was discovered in a meadow at Foleshill, belonging to Mr Jos. Whiting, of that place, in digging a trench, about two feet below the surface, an earthen pot, containing upwards of 1,800 Roman copper coins, principally of the Emperors Constantine, Constans, Constantius and Magentius; most of which remain in the possession of Mr Whiting, for the inspection of the curious. And on Sunday last, in continuing the same trench, he found another earthen jug, containing a greater quantity of larger coin; but the latter are in greater preservation.

The discovery of this hoard at Bullester Fields Farm is interesting, for the person who buried it presumably intended to return, so its burial place needed to be identifiable; somewhere near a known trackway and not in the middle of thick forest. To the west of the hoard site lies Barrs Hill in Radford, where in the last century a small number of Roman coins and pottery were found. One local legend states that the Roman general Agricola stopped here, built an encampment on Barrs Hill and named the nearby settlement Coventina. The interest of this legend lies in the fact that Coventina, a Celtic–Roman water goddess, was virtually unknown in this country until her only known shrine was discovered at Carrawburgh in Yorkshire in the 1890s. Coventina, being a water goddess, would have been at home in Coventry with its rivers, pools and springs: she was depicted naked or half naked holding a plant, and pouring water from a jug or urn. An ancient coin-like object was discovered near the Priory Mill in New Buildings in the last century. This had on one side a woman pouring water from a jug, and on the other a naked woman with a flower at her feet. It is possible that this has some connection with the legend.

During the last century, while digging near Cross Cheaping, workmen unearthed a 10 in high marble statuette. Described as a figure hugging a wheatsheaf and leaning on a shield, this is obviously a representation of Mars in his two roles as god of agriculture, indicated by the wheatsheaf, and god of war, shown by the shield. William Fretton, a local historian in the last century, stated that he had found several Roman coins around the same area, including Broadgate Hill. The father of Coventry's modern archaeology, John Bailey Shelton, discovered a wooden causeway, 200 yards long and 15 ft wide between Silver Street and Palmer Lane. It was well constructed and considered by Shelton at least to be Roman, as were the remains of a boat he excavated in Broadgate. He also uncovered two Roman horseshoes on the site of the old gas showrooms (now Equity and Law) in Corporation Street. More important was Shelton's excavation work in the river in Cox Street. He removed 6 ft of rubble from the river bed and found in the original gravel-bed of the river 'a coin of Emperor Gallienus, AD 253–68, a bronze ring, jet ring, toilet set for nails and ears, surgeons' needles, pottery, iron handles, bronze for beating out, shears, and a variety of other objects.' All of the objects were sent to the British Museum. The smaller objects were said to have been 'the contents of a Roman lady's satchel'.

Other Roman finds include coins of Tiberius Caesar (AD 14) and Roman pottery, found in Radford in 1961; vases near Broad Lane and Stoke; possible pottery kilns at Geoffrey Wood Cross in Stoke; and coins and pottery from Keresley, Coundon, Walsgrave and Stoke. Another local legend connects the district with the late Roman Saint Quientan: a possible surviving connection is Quinton Pool in Cheylesmore, between Coventry and Baginton. The pool was supposed to have been named after the medieval keeper of Cheylesmore Park, Thomas Quinton, but perhaps he was named after the pool.

Sometime before the eighth century, people began to settle in the area in greater numbers. Antiquarians have suggested the earliest site of habitation was around Barrs Hill (the site of the legendary Roman camp). Others place the settlement in the valley between Barrs Hill and Broadgate Hill. While excavating around Corporation Street, Shelton discovered a very early boat, cut out of a single tree trunk, which may be early British. This boat once carried someone across the long-gone 'Babba-lacu', a large lake stretching from where is now Hill and Hales Street to half-way up what was Smithford Street (now part of the precinct). At its narrowest the lake was about 200 yards wide.

With a much wider River Sherbourne and a large pool covering Pool Meadow and Swanswell Pool, early settlers were never short of water and game, which attracted them to the site in the first place.

What name these early settlers used had been the cause of much speculation. An early spelling comes from a confirmation charter of Coventry Priory, dating from the 1040s. 'Couaentree' is said to mean 'the town on the Cune', Cune being the original name of the Sherbourne. By the mid-1060s the spelling is recorded as 'Cofantreo' and this form is used by modern place-name experts to trace the name's original meaning. 'Cofa-treo' translates as 'Cofa's treo', or the tree of Cofa. This suggests a tree was considered important in the early settlement, but Cofa's connection to the tree is less easily explained. Cofa may have been the name of a settler, or may have some connection with pagan tree worship: it could possibly be the name of a deity. Another translation, 'Covent-tre', means 'the town of the convent', referring to St Osburg's nunnery. Medieval chroniclers are notorious for their inconsistent spellings, so we also find the city referred to as 'Couentre', 'Coventrev', 'Coventria', for example. Despite all this confusion, however, it is now generally accepted that Coventry derives from 'Cofa's tree'.

Many religions were still practised in England long after the establishment of the Church, the new faith having difficulty superceding the old. Pope Gregory the Great in AD 601 decreed that as many remaining heathen customs as possible should be converted into Christian observances. Heathen deities were to be converted into Christian saints if necessary. Apart from Cofa, other pagan survivals in early Coventry were the fertility ritual now associated with Lady Godiva (chapter two) and well and spring worship, especially that connected with Hobs Hole, Emma's Well and St Catherine's Well. Hobs Hole was a spring-fed walled pool which lay near what is now Cox Street. It is interesting because Hob was a name once given to the devil himself. It is also interesting and significant that Hobs Hole had a ceremony attached to it which took place after the yearly election of the mayor of Hobs Hole. The new mayor was taken to the small pool and forcibly submerged in the water, an event reminiscent of ancient pagan sacrifices to water gods where victims were drowned as offerings. This ceremony, which lasted into the nineteenth century, may have been a vague memory of this ancient and more disturbing tradition.

Emma's Well, a paved well once to be found near Whitefriars, had no surviving ceremonies attached to it, but the name 'Emma' must have had some local significance as it is remembered in the rhyme:

> Ride a cock-horse to Coventry Cross,
> To see what Emma can buy,
> A penny white cake I'll buy for her sake,
> And a two-penny tart or a pie.

This rhyme, which predates the Banbury Cross rhyme, is thought to have pagan connections. The cock-horse is a pre-Roman fertility symbol, while the white cake may be connected with the choosing of sacrificial victims – the person who picked the burnt portion was the sacrifice. St Catherine's Well, in today's Beaumont Crescent, was an ancient pre-Christian sacred spring which was later dedicated to a Christian saint, according to Pope Gregory's decree. In this instance St Catherine herself was also made Christian, for she was originally a pagan deity – her wheel being an ancient symbol of the sun.

As stated earlier, Cofa may have some connection with tree worship, and there have been speculations that there was a sacred oak in the area we now call Broadgate. Sacred oaks were later either turned into Gospel Oaks or were condemned as 'devils' or 'blasted' oaks. No reference to ancient tree groves survives within the city, but one did last into the eighteenth century. This was probably in the Great Park near the present London Road cemetery. What is known today as The Grove, near the memorial park, was also once a tree grove of ancient date. The Church dealt with this pagan remnant by placing a stone cross there. Known as the New or Queen's Cross, it was still standing in 1630.

Another custom which took place in Coventry at least until the sixteenth century was the annual night-time parade of two giant wicker figures with candles on their heads. Nowhere in English history can wicker giants be found except in Celtic ceremonial sacrifices. It is alleged that the Celts constructed huge wicker figures, placed their chosen victims inside and burned them. The Coventry wicker giants with their burning heads can only be a memory of this long-dead ceremony.

The arrival of Christianity in Coventry is marked by the strange legend that the Saint of Cologne brought 11,000 virgins to the settlement, but no more details are given. Another legend tells of St Chad and his erection of a chapel here, on Barrs Hill, near St Nicholas Street. Around AD 700 the holy virgin St Osburg established a nunnery in Coventry and became its first abbess. St Osburg is an obscure figure of whom virtually nothing is known. She was first mentioned by St Aldhelm, Bishop of Sherborne (d. AD 709) in his *De laudibus virginitatis*, written around AD 675. His book, dedicated to the Sisterhood of Barking, praises the holy virgins of that place and among their names he records that of the holy virgin 'Osburga'. Osburg, along with others of her sisterhood, left Barking and established new holy houses across the land. She remained abbess of the Coventry nunnery after its foundation until she died a saint. Her remains thereafter were placed in a shrine in its church. This first holy establishment is thought to have stood somewhere between today's Palmer Lane and Hill Top. Most holy houses and churches were built directly on top of pagan sites, their inmates actively mingling with the local community.

Later, the nunnery was rebuilt in stone and continued its active quest in suppressing and utilizing paganism in early Coventry. All was well until 1016 when the *Anglo-Saxon Chronicle* states: 'In this year came Cnut with his host and with him ealdorman Eadric, and crossed the Thames into Mercia at Cricklade, and then, during the season of Christmas, turned into Warwickshire, and harried and burned and slew all they found.' John Rous, priest and antiquary, later added to this extract that 'even the Abbey of Nuns at Coventry is destroyed, of which in times past the Virgin St Osburg was the abbess.' This 'host' of invaders, the Danish Canute and Saxon turncoat Edric the Traitor, rampaged throughout England, harried by the Saxons all the way, and after many skirmishes defeated the newly crowned King Edmund. Canute thereafter became King of England through force of arms.

This was not the first Danish invasion of the area, for England had been harried by them in earlier times. England seemed lost to the Danes until King Alfred the Great forced the invaders to agree to the Peace of Wedmore (AD 878), which confined them to the Danelaw, an area to the east of Watling Street. The Danelaw had an ill defined frontier and two places in Coventry have names of Danish origin; namely Biggin in Stoke (biggin is Danish for building) and Keresley in the north ('Kaerer's clearing'). Coventry's once famous Hock Tuesday Play, a pseudo-battle, was supposed to commemorate the massacre of all the Danes living in England by order of the king, on St Brice's Day in 1002.

A possible relic of the attack on the nunnery is a fragment of tenth-century decorated Saxon cross which was found in Palmer Lane during the construction of Trinity Street in 1936. It is thought to have been broken down by the invaders. A Danish or Viking axe has also been found. When King Canute sat safely on the throne of England he began to repair many holy houses that his army had sacked during the invasion. St Osburg's nunnery benefited perhaps from this act, and continued its life as an important religious centre. Early pilgrims came here to visit the shrine of the virgin saint, and in 1022 Archbishop Aethelnoth presented a much worshipped and holy relic to the nuns, namely the arm of St Augustine of Hippo. The relic had been pur-

Victorian illustration showing the dress of a Saxon abbess. Coventry's St Osburg probably looked something like this

This Saxon cross fragment of about the tenth century shows what is thought to be a squirrel amid typical Saxon decorative work. It is one of the largest items to survive from Saxon Coventry

chased by order of Canute in the city of Pavia for 100 talents of gold and 100 talents of silver while he was returning from a pilgrimage to Rome. It was considered that presenting the relic would gain the king 'many friends and prayers'. This additional relic would form the basis of a collection which would be worshipped by pilgrims into the early sixteenth century. The days of the nunnery, however, were numbered, for in the year 1042 the nuns were ordered to leave. The only place in the settlement thereafter to bear the name of the founding holy virgin was St Osburg's Pool, now Pool Meadow.

CHAPTER TWO

Leofric and Godiva

F rom the year 1043 most events in Coventry's history are documented. It was also at this time that Leofric, Earl of Mercia and his wife, Lady Godiva (Godgifu) made their appearance. Leofric's foundation of the Benedictine Priory of St Mary (chapter three) on 4 October of this year was an important event in Coventry's early history.

Earl Leofric, along with Earl Godwin of Wessex and Earl Siward of Northumbria, was one of the most powerful noblemen in England. A close friend and confidant of King Edward the Confessor, Leofric was noted for his wisdom and piety, but also an iron fist, which he showed during a revolt in Worcestershire, when Worcester was razed to the ground. Leofric helped to raise three monarchs (Harold I, Harthacnut and Edward the Confessor) to the throne and was considered an uncanonized saint, for it is said that a vision of Christ had appeared before him and Edward the Confessor.

Godiva, born around AD 1000, was powerful and rich in her own rights and was the sister of Thorold, Sheriff of Lincolnshire. She was described as a woman of great beauty, with hair flowing down beyond her waist. Her life was devoted to the worship of the Virgin Mary, and she endowed many churches with gifts.

Leofric and Godiva lived at Kings Bromley in Staffordshire, and although there are no records to show they came to Coventry, in all likelihood they were regular visitors, with their own quarters within the priory walls. The earliest account of Godiva's famous ride to relieve Coventry of excessive taxes was written by Roger of Wendover (historian of St Albans from 1188 to 1236) in his *Flores Historiarum* ('Flowers of History'). This is what his original version of the legend said:

The Countess, wishing in a most pious spirit to deliver the city of Coventry from a burdensome and most shameful bondage, often entreated the Count, her husband, with earnest prayers, to deliver the city from the bondage of which I have spoken. The Count

A romanticised Victorian statuette of Coventry's world famous Lady Godiva. The lady's ride is now thought to have been the memory of an ancient fertility ritual

reproached her for persevering in asking a thing that would be injurious to him, and at last charged her never again to mention the subject to him. But she continued to urge on her husband the same request, and at last received this answer from him: 'Mount your horse, naked, and ride through the town from beginning to end at a time when all the people are assembled and when you return you shall obtain what you ask,' and the Countess answered: 'If I am willing to do this, will you give me permission?' The Count replied, 'I will.' Then the Countess Godiva, beloved by God, on a set day, mounted her horse, naked, letting fall her hair and so covering her whole body, her white legs only showing; and attended by two knights she rode through the market seen by none. And when she finished her journey, she returned with joy to her husband, who looked on this as a miracle. And Count Leofric, releasing the city of Coventry from bondage, confirmed the charter which he gave with the sanction of his own seal.

No other early chronicles contain any reference to the ride although Godiva and Leofric are often mentioned. It was not until the early fourteenth century onwards that a version of Wendover's story reappeared, and other versions sprang forth. It is thought that when the monks of Coventry were evicted by their bishop in 1190 some went to St Albans. When they told Roger of Godiva's supposed ride, he added this 'monkish' story to his history.

Wendover's account, on which the whole legend is based, gives the idea that Leofric was a hard unjust man, and the idea of him forcing his wife, one of the highest ranking ladies in England, to carry out such an act is simply unbelievable. A similar event is described as having taken place in St Briavels in Gloucestershire. In his *History of Gloucestershire* (1779), Samuel Rudder tells of the Earl of Herefordshire in the time of King John, who allowed his wife to ride naked so that the people of the village would gain the right to gather wood.

What the Godiva legend seems to be is the result of the monks of Coventry attaching an old pagan fertility ritual to a pious lady many years after her death, using her as a symbol of self-sacrifice. Godiva's ride appears to be based on one of the fertility ceremonies which were once common throughout England. Our ancestors considered horses and naked women to be powerful fertility symbols, and the Celtic goddess Epona was often depicted as a naked woman on horseback. A ceremony which used to take place at Southam, south of Coventry, at the beginning of this century is an interesting parallel. Southam also had what is called a Godiva procession, with two Godivas, one black and one white, both representing the lady. Images or figures would be used or, as in the nineteenth century, a black woman would be specially brought in to play the part. The black Godiva may originate in the fertility rites which Pliny describes, when Celtic women blackened their bodies with woad. It is also worth remembering that in some parts of the world ancient black goddesses survive into the present as black madonnas. One version of the Banbury Cross rhyme recorded in 1863 goes thus:

> Ride a cock-horse to Banbury Cross,
> To see a black lady ride on a white horse.

These black and white Godivas are thought to represent summer and winter, light and darkness, life and death. The Southam Godivas were led by a man wearing a horned mask called Brazen Face, a brother to the Dorset Ooser and many other bull-faced men once used in cere-

The figure of St George which has been used to represent Peeping Tom since 1659. It now stands in Cathedral Lanes overlooking Lady Godiva's statue

monies throughout England and said to represent fertility and the sun. Their use goes back to prehistory, and their image survived despite papal decrees for their banishment.

The other aspect of the Godiva ride, Peeping Tom, does not belong with the original Godiva legend, as his inclusion came at a much later date. Recent evidence suggests that the legend may have originated with the council's earliest commission of a Godiva painting in 1586. When this painting was being cleaned in 1976, under the layers of grime a figure of a bearded man looking from an upper-storey window came to light. This discovery may make the Peeping Tom legend more ancient than previously thought, or the artist may have meant the figure to represent Leofric, despite the legend that Godiva rode unobserved.

The oak figure we now call Peeping Tom, standing in Cathedral Lanes, has been used to represent Tom since at least 1659, when it looked from a window in Cross Cheaping. In 1678 Alderman Owen moved the figure to Greyfriars Lane and later, around 1775, city antiquarian Thomas Sharp had it removed to his shop in Smithford Street. This shop later became the corner shop, and Tom was placed in a special corner window looking down Hertford Street. In the 1870s the Kings Head was rebuilt, taking in the corner, and Tom was moved to that building; here he remained until the outbreak of the Second World War. Tom reappeared after the war in the Hotel Leofric, before moving in 1991 to his present site, overlooking the statue of Godiva. The figure itself is a fifteenth-century representation of St George and probably originally held a spear and stood astride a dragon. It probably originated in St Mary's Priory or St George's chapel in Gosford Street. Local legend states that St George was born and died in Coventry, and his father Lord Albert is commemorated by the local River Albert. Thomas Percy, Bishop of Dromore, in his *Reliques of Ancient English Poetry* reprints an ancient poem recounting St George's adventures which ends as follows:

> Where being in a short space arrived,
> Unto his native dwelling place;
> Therein with his dear love he lived,
> And fortune did his nuptials grace;
> They many years of joy did see,
> And led their lives at Coventree.

In 1057 the *Anglo-Saxon Chronicle* records, 'In this same year, on 30 October, Earl Leofric passed away. He was very wise in all matters, both religious and secular, that benefited all this nation.' He died at his hall in Kings Bromley. Leofric's burial, however, took place with great pomp and solemnity at St Mary's Priory in Coventry, that he and Godiva had founded.

After Leofric's death Godiva probably moved to Evesham, where she resided until her own death on 10 September 1067 (as recorded in the Douce Manuscript at Oxford). Lady Godiva died as England was in turmoil following Duke William's victory at Hastings. Many Saxon nobles like her own son Aelfgar, Earl of Mercia, became outlaws using guerrilla warfare against the invaders. It was due to this turmoil that Godiva was originally buried in Holy Trinity church in Evesham. Later, however, when William the Conqueror controlled England, her remains were re-interred next to the great Saxon earl in St Mary's Priory.

The Coventry Godiva knew is partly revealed by the Domesday Survey of 1086, which gives an idea of Coventry's population after the positive influence of the foundation of the monastery. The king had passed Godiva's land to Nicholas, Sheriff of Staffordshire; the lands of the priory were not included in the survey. The Domesday entry reads thus:

> The Countess held Couentrev. There are five hides. The arable employs twenty ploughs. Three are in the demesne, and seven bond-men [tenant farmers owing some service to the lord of the manor]. There are fifty villeins [workers bonded to the lord] and twelve bordars [cottagers] with twenty ploughs. A mill pays 3 shillings. Wood two miles long and the same broad. In King Edward's time and afterwards it was worth twelve pounds by weight. These lands of the Countess Godiva, Nicholas holds to farm of the King.

The population in the survey amounts to around 350, including children. An estimate for the full population, including the priory's half, is over 1,000, making it a fairly large community by eleventh-century standards.

CHAPTER THREE

St Mary's Priory

S t Mary's monastery, which Leofric founded on 4 October 1043 grew into one of the richest religious houses in England. The later thirteenth-century priory church measured 425 ft in length by the fifteenth century, dwarfing the old cathedral. This huge monastic house is now gone, its only remains being pillars, a tower base and stonework, which can be seen at both ends of Priory Row.

The Benedictine monastery for an abbot and twenty-four monks was dedicated by Edsi, Archbishop of Canterbury, to God, the Virgin Mary, St Peter, St Osburg and All Saints. During this dedication ceremony Earl Leofric laid his founding charter upon the newly consecrated altar, which not only granted the foundation, but also gave lordship over twenty-four villages for the maintenance of the house. Of this first church nothing remains but the written word. In it were rehoused the relics of St Osburg and the arm of St Augustine. Godiva took special interest in the church, endowing it with many gifts in honour of the Virgin Mary. Chroniclers tell that Godiva had all her gold and silver melted down and made into crosses, images of saints and other decorations to grace her favoured house of God. William of Malmesbury states that 'it was enriched and beautified with so much gold and silver that the walls seemed too narrow to contain it.' On her death bed, Godiva gave a heavy gem-encrusted gold chain to the monastery, directing that it should be placed around the neck of the image of the Virgin. Those who came to pray, she stated, should say a prayer for each stone in the chain.

Fourteen years after its foundation, Earl Leofric was laid in state within the monastery walls. Later his warrior son, Aelfgar, who once brought a Welsh army into England and sacked Hereford and its minster, killing the clergy, was finally laid to rest here in 1052, less than a year after regaining his title of Earl of Mercia. Aelfgar was paid off as he was thought to be a threat to the king.

Life at the Benedictine monastery was prosperous and uneventful until the arrival of the notorious Robert de Limesey, Bishop of Chester. He had obtained the custody of the monastery after the death of the abbot in 1095, and by papal decree moved his seat from Chester

This Victorian engraving, based on an ancient manuscript decoration, shows a scene once common in Coventry's great priory church

to Coventry, which was a wealthier place. Thus he became the first Bishop of Coventry, taking over the role of the abbot. De Limesey placed a prior in charge, thereby turning the monastery into a priory, and the church into a cathedral. Coventry had now technically become a city. As he settled into his new bishopric, Limesey began to bleed it: he entered the monks' dormitory with armed men and broke open their chests in search of valuables, and proceeded to have buildings pulled down and the materials carried off for his own use. Soon his attention was drawn to the priory cathedral. Here he pillaged the shrines which the monastery had been building up over a number of years, and from one beam in the church scraped 500 marks-worth of silver. All this was done despite the protests of the monks, who were practically reduced to paupers. When Limesey died in 1117 his remains were laid to rest by the monks, in the cathedral that he had so vigorously pillaged.

Five other bishops followed Limesey, one of whom later built the bishop's palace, which stood near the present new cathedral. In 1185 the bishop's seat was moved to Lichfield (where originally it had been after 1066) and the bishop took the title of Bishop of Coventry and

Lichfield. The diocese was renamed the Diocese of Lichfield and Coventry in 1668. It remained so until 1837 when Coventry and the surrounding Warwickshire parishes became an archdeaconry of the Diocese of Worcester.

In 1184, Henry II gave the bishopric to his friend Hugh de Novant, a clerk. Novant had a lust for power and wealth, and a great dislike for monks. After the accession of Richard I in 1189, the king, needing money to finance his crusade, sold the priory to Novant for 300 marks. Novant's oppressive behaviour towards the monks and his gradual acquisition of priory lands came to a head when the monks tried to stand up to him, and he laid charges against them. On his next visit to the priory, he was physically attacked by the enraged monks, who split his head open with the altar crucifix. Novant accused them of assault and desecration, and the monks, by order of the Archbishop of Canterbury, were removed from the priory. Dispossessed, the brothers left Coventry and went to other houses. Nearly five years passed before King Richard returned to England and, hearing of Novant's misdeeds, threw him out of office. A group of monks went to Rome to try to gain back their priory, which they eventually succeeded in doing. This was not the first time that the monks had been evicted, for in 1143 Earl Robert Marmion of Tamworth, a 'man great in warr', threw the monks out and fortified the priory (chapter four).

It is thought that Coventry Priory was rebuilt in the late thirteenth century and the present remains, which are Early English in style, date from this period. Tradition states that Leofric and Godiva were re-interred in the church's choir. This second church, cloisters, accommodation, outbuildings and gardens took in a large area of land within the present Priory Row, Trinity Street, Pool Meadow (which then fed the priory's mill) and Priory Street. Its stone gatehouse stood before a courtyard in front of the west entrance, some of which still remains between Priory Row and New Buildings. The site of the priory gatehouse is now H. Samuel's in Trinity Street.

The priory church, completed in the late fourteenth to early fifteenth century, is generally accepted as having three spires, like Lichfield. Some people think, however, that it looked like Salisbury or Canterbury. The theory of a triple-spired church is based on an old seal, its legend mostly obliterated, which shows a bishop standing before a church with three spires. This building is thought by some to be Coventry Priory, although it is just as likely to be Lichfield, as the joint diocese had the bishop's seat at Lichfield. Salisbury, unlike Lichfield, was built in the same period and is generally very close in size to the priory church. Salisbury also has three spires, although

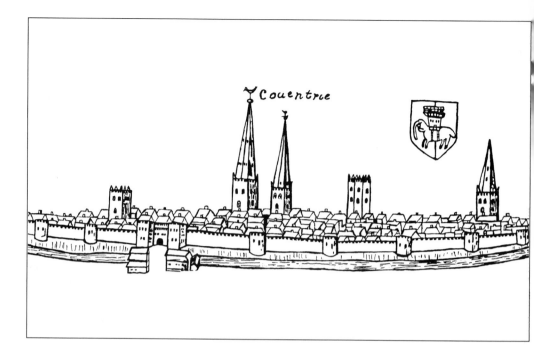

those on the west end are smaller and squatter than Lichfield. There is another seal attributed to the priory which shows a building similar to Canterbury, but medieval seals are notoriously unreliable when depicting architectural styles.

There is no description of the church in existence; all that does remain is one distant view of Coventry showing, among its spires, a solitary tower. The drawing comes from a book published in 1588 by William Smith, Rouge Dragon Pursuivant Herald to Queen Elizabeth I. In his book, entitled *A Particuler Description of England*, he sketched Coventry with its buildings within the city walls. Each tower and spire is shown in the right place, and next to Trinity church can be seen a tower, surmounted with pinnacles. It has been suggested that this is the central tower of the priory church still standing fifty-eight years after its demolition was ordered. If one looks closely, however, it can be seen that this is not a square tower, but a building in three vertical sections with narrow windows. This 'central tower' may be, in fact, the west entrance of the church, part of which still remains between New Buildings and Priory Row. It originally consisted of four joined octagonal towers, standing on either side of the entrance. Two octagonal tower bases still remain, but the rest was demolished before the Revd John Bryan built houses here in 1648. The windows seen in Smith's sketch, however, can still be seen. Knowing the importance of

A rare view of walled Coventry copied from a drawing by William Smith, Rouge Dragon Pursuivant Herald to Elizabeth I, from his *Particuler Description of England* printed in 1588

these remains, Smith appears to have exaggerated their height in this otherwise fairly accurate sketch.

Coventry Priory was a great place of pilgrimage, for it contained numerous relics within its walls. In a document entitled 'The Inventorie of all manner of Reliques conteyned in the Cathedrall Church of Coventrie', they are named: a shrine of St Osburg of copper; St Osburg's head closed in copper and gilt; a part of the Holy Cross held in silver and gilt; a relic of Thomas à Becket of Canterbury; a piece of Our Lady's Tomb; a relic of St Cecily's foot; a cross with a relic of St James, silver and gilt and set with stones; an image of St George, with a bone of his shielded in silver; an arm of St Justin, in silver; an arm of St Jerome, in silver; an arm of St Augustine, in silver; a relic of St Andrew; a rib of St Laurence in silver; an arm of St Sibiyne; a relic of St Catherine; a barrel of relics of confessors; four little crosses, of copper; two bags of relics; and finally a phial of Our Lady's milk in a silver and gilt reliquary. These important relics placed Coventry on the route of many an English pilgrim. Pilgrims' badges from Canterbury and as far away as St James' shrine in Spain

Coventry Priory housed many relics, including the venerated arm of St Augustine of Hippo. Such relics brought pilgrims flocking to the city. Based on a manuscript illustration

were found many years ago in the Sherbourne in Palmer Lane. There were reports of miracle healings at the shrine of St Osburg, and the bishop (whose name is not recorded) ordered that her day be kept on 23 January. In 1462 her relics were placed in a larger more elaborate shrine in a more prominent part of the church. A hostel was set up by the Benedictines in Palmer Lane, and the priory's guest-house, a large timbered building, became known as the Pilgrims' Rest. Here the pilgrim (or palmer) could be well watered and fed, as these houses were some of the finest inns of the period. The Pilgrims' Rest was demolished in 1820, and replaced with a brick building, itself demolished in 1936 when Trinity Street was being constructed.

The priory and its cathedral church were dissolved during the reign of Henry VIII. He had stayed at the priory only a few years before his break with Rome, and the consequent dissolution of monastic houses throughout England. In 1539 Thomas Cromwell sent agents to assess Coventry Priory, Greyfriars, Whitefriars, Charterhouse and St John's. The Prior of Coventry pleaded for his house, and Bishop Rowland Lee of Coventry and Lichfield wrote to Cromwell, who wrote back assuring the survival of the church. Despite this assurance the king's agent returned to Coventry and the bishop once again put pen to paper:

My singular Good Lord Cromwell,

My duty remembered unto your good lordship; it may please the same to call unto your lordship's remembrance, my suit made to your lordship, for the Cathedral Church of Coventry, for the continuance of

The Pilgrim's Rest in Palmer Lane began life as a monastic guest house for pilgrims. After the dissolution it became an ordinary tavern

the same, that, upon alteration, it might stand. Whereunto your lordship did give the loving answer of comfort, and now I am informed
by the letters herein enclosed, from the Mayor and Aldermen of the
City, that Dr Loudon repairs hither for the suppression of the same.

My good Lord, help me and the city both, in this, and that the
church may stand, whereby I may keep my name, and the city have
commodity and ease to their desire, which shall follow if, by your
goodness it might be brought to a Collegiate Church, as Lichfield,
and so that the poor city shall have perpetual comfort of the same,
as knoweth the Holy Trinity who preserve your Lordship in honour
to your heart's comfort.

Despite this final plea, and despite Lichfield's reprieve, the cathedral church and priory were taken by the Crown on 15 January 1539. Dr
Loudon wrote to Cromwell that Thomas Camswell, the prior, was 'a
sad honest priest as his neighbours do report him, and a Bachelor of
Divinity. He gave his house unto the King's grace willingly, and in
like manner did all his brethren.' The prior and his brother monks
gathered their belongings and left the priory for ever, after being part
of the city for nearly 500 years. As they passed their once busy guest-
house in Palmer Lane, one of these black-robed monks may have
thrown the priory keys into the river, for in 1852 a large bunch of keys
such as would have been used there were dredged out of the
Sherbourne.

The end of the priory was a disaster for the city's growth and prosperity, which had been faltering since 1500. The population, which
was around 10,000, fell to 3,000 through lack of trade and commerce.
This great religious centre was in a state of shock, for it lost not only
the priory, but also the large monastic houses of the Franciscans at
Greyfriars, the Carmelites at Whitefriars and the Carthusians at the
Charterhouse. The buildings were turned into stone quarries, and in no
time the great and beautiful cathedral was reduced to rubble, leaving
only the west entrance and a few walls and outbuildings standing. The
land was sold to the City Corporation, while other assets were granted
to prominent citizens such as John Hales, who turned Whitefriars into
his own private house. So ended the great priory, which for centuries
had stood in the centre of Coventry, with Holy Trinity and St
Michael's constituting a scene unequalled in the land.

CHAPTER FOUR

Defensive Ditches and the Castle

C oventry had two defensive ditches before the walls were built, making the settlement into a 'bury' or lowland hill-fort. The ditches were known as the Hyrsum, Anglo-Saxon for forced obedience, and the Red Ditch. Both constitute somewhat of a mystery, but are obviously major defensive works. The ditches completely surrounded the settlement, taking in some agricultural land as well. It may have been used by nearby settlements as a place of refuge in troubled times.

The Hyrsum stretched from the bottom of what is now Gosford Street, running about a hundred yards in, but parallel with Gosford, Jordan Well, Earl and High Street. It then curved inwards through Hertford Street, by Shelton Square and into Market Way. This course has been archaeologically investigated, but the rest of the route is sup-

The Red Ditch and Hyrsum Ditch in their day may have looked something like this, a flooded ditch surmounted by a wooden palisade

position: it probably continued down Smithford Way, turning into the natural hollow and areas of water which lay along Corporation, Hales and Fairfax Streets and curving round into Gosford Street. It is not unlikely that this and later ditches were palisaded.

The Red Ditch may have been an inner perimeter ditch, working as a second layer of defence. This ditch in most places is 25 ft deep, cut into the bedrock, and 21 ft across. A section of the Red Ditch was excavated in Broadgate and dated to the twelfth century, but finds of tenth-century Stamford ware nearby suggest it is much older. The ditch ran from Greyfriars Lane, cut through the corner of Broadgate, down Bayley Lane and crossed Jordan Well to join up with the Hyrsum on its south side. There is evidence that this particular fortification may have been more extensive, but archaeological exploration to prove this can be difficult in a modern city. During recent excavations in Bayley Lane, part of this ditch came to light; its direction, however, did not fit in with its generally accepted position, adding to the mystery of the Red Ditch. Excavations in available areas may cause confusion, for they may show predecessors of the final defences.

Occasionally referred to as the Castle Ditch, the Red Ditch was once thought to constitute the defences of Coventry Castle, but although it was in the vicinity of the castle, the acreage it takes in is far too large. Perhaps the Red Ditch was a predecessor or development of the Hyrsum, or it may have constituted a secondary internal defence, similar to those found in Norman motte and bailey castles.

Coventry Castle had a short but eventful history. Its main entrance was in or through Broadgate, the 'Brod-yate'. As for the castle itself, it probably stood between Bayley Lane, High Street and Earl Street. Parts of it may still exist as the undervaults and parts of Caesar's Tower (rebuilt after the war) of St Mary's Hall. The building of the castle was initially undertaken by the Earls of Chester who inherited part of Coventry through marriage to a descendant of Earl Leofric. The south side of the city, which later became St Michael's parish, was known as the Earl's Half, with the north half, Trinity parish, known as the Prior's Half, as the priory and its land stood there.

Much has been said in the past about Coventry being a divided city, but in reality these divisions were not particularly rigid. The city had two landowners, the earl and the prior, but despite the separate administration of the two areas, the main decisions of law were taken in St Michael's churchyard at a meeting called the portmanmoot, the decisions of which affected the whole city. In 1250 the Prior of Coventry gained the earl's half of the city, except Cheylesmore manor house and park by deed of gift and concord from Roger and Cecily de

Montalt (Cecily was a descendant of Ranulf, last Earl of Chester). Over the years that followed the people of Coventry grew to resent the prior's power, even trying to kill him by witchcraft. The prior tried to take control of the portmanmoot but was always resisted. An end to the power struggle came in sight when Queen Isabella inherited Cheylesmore in 1330 and set about breaking the prior's monopoly in the city: she began to seize land in 1335 claiming that the prior had no licence to hold it. The prior felt his power slipping away and threatened to divide the city by setting up his own moot and trade centres. The beginning of the end of the power struggle came with the Charter of Incorporation in 1345, obviously pressed forward by Isabella giving the men of Coventry the right to elect their own mayor and bailiffs. The prior's wings were finally clipped in 1335 with the Tripartite Indenture, in which he formally relinquished many of his earlier claims and much of his power.

After the death of Henry I in 1135, Stephen of Blois, nephew of Henry, crossed the channel and seized the throne of England. The following year Matilda, the daughter of the late king, made claim to the crown. The barons of England were split, thus beginning a bloody and savage civil war which lasted for eighteen years. The Earls of Chester took the side of Matilda in the war. It has been said in the past that the prior and monks of Coventry Priory supported King Stephen, but this seems unlikely, as to do this in the face of such a powerful enemy would threaten their very existence in Coventry, and Earl Marmion supported the king yet threw the monks out. In 1137 the *Anglo-Saxon Chronicle* records that as the conflict with Stephen spiralled, 'every great man built him castles and held them against the King; and they filled the whole land with these castles. They sorely burdened the unhappy people of the country with forced labour on the castles.' Coventry Castle was built with this forced labour by the warlord Earl Ranulf Gernons. Ditched and palisaded, with its keep on an artificial mound, the wooden stronghold was to be the scene of several violent exchanges during the forthcoming civil war.

The first to come in the king's name to take Coventry Castle was Earl Robert Marmion of Tamworth. Marmion, noted as being 'great in warr', arrived with a large group of knights and burst into the monastery, driving all the monks out. Over the following weeks he fortified the church and had a network of defensive ditches and mantraps dug. On 8 September 1143 Earl Ranulf of Chester and his force sallied forth from the castle to meet him. Marmion and his men left the monastery and waited among the ditches; then with a typical act of bravado, Marmion rode forward alone and paraded up and down before his enemies. This audacity ended when the warrior's horse fell

A Victorian engraving showing the keep of a Norman castle. Coventry Castle was probably of a similar design

into one of his own mantraps. As the great Earl Marmion of Tamworth fell, a soldier of Earl Ranulf dashed forward and beheaded him.

In 1145 Earl Ranulf found himself taken in battle and imprisoned by King Stephen, who seized Coventry Castle. The following year Ranulf was released, and gathered a force together to retake the castle. The earl and his men arrived in Coventry, and soon discovered that Earl Marmion III (Robert's brother) held the castle and that the king was on his way to relieve it. A force placed the castle under a state of siege, and Ranulf had a siege tower built, while others rode to harry and attack the king's army when and wherever it had the chance. The earl's men took some of the king's men prisoner, and put others to flight. The king himself was wounded and for a short time put out of action. These skirmishes eventually ended in favour of the king, and Earl Ranulf fled when Stephen entered Coventry. The king proceeded to dismantle the castle, but it was restored in stone by Hugh of Chester, who held the lordship after Earl Ranulf was poisoned. His charter refers to the 'broadgate of my castle' (from which Broadgate gets its name). Earl Hugh, with some of his Coventry men, left the city in 1173 to fight against Henry II in the Barons' Revolt. For this the people of Coventry were punished when the revolt failed the following year. The loss of the city's liberties were returned six years later.

Earl Hugh's successor, Earl Ranulf Blundeville, Duke of Brittany, and the last Earl of Chester and Richmond, died in 1232 without male issue, and the castle was passed on by marriage to Roger de Montalt, who granted part of his lordship to the prior to finance his part in the third crusade. At this point the castle appears to have been in a fairly ruinous condition, probably as its defences had been destroyed by order of King John. To make up for this, a moated manor house with gardens, orchards and walls, had been erected at Cheylesmore, set within a park. Robert de Montalt (Roger's grandson) died without issue and passed the Cheylesmore estate to Queen Isabella and John de Eltham. When the latter died, the queen acquired the whole estate and later granted it to Edward the Black Prince, whose three feathers appear among our civic heraldry.

Remains of Coventry Castle still existed in the sixteenth century, for when Mary Queen of Scots was incarcerated here she had to be held at The Black Bull and St Mary's Hall as it was found 'impossible to lodge her within the old castle remains'. The chronicler John Stowe described what remained of the city's once important castle as 'a fort-let or pile standing in Earls Street'. This 'pile', probably the remains of the castle's keep, then disappeared from the records, so Coventry Castle was no more.

CHAPTER FIVE

Prosperity and Plague

n the year 1200 Coventry was dominated by the priory, its church and the castle. Between these lay the chapels of St Michael and Holy Trinity, and around all lay the thirteenth-century settlement surrounded by the Hyrsum and Red Ditch.

The town was prosperous and growing, having its own market outside the priory gate in Cross Cheaping, and a fair (held in Broadgate) was granted in 1217. Charters granted before and after 1200 gave the town the status of borough. The burgesses held their land by fee burgage, paying land rent and owing no service to their lord. They also had the right to hold their own portmanmoot and elect their own judicial officers.

An industry probably introduced by the monks had far-reaching effects on the town, and was ultimately responsible for Coventry growing wealthy and becoming the third largest city in medieval England. The basis for this prosperity was wool. Coventry also produced metalwork and leather goods, but it was wool weaving and the cloth trade which financed the city's growth for the next 400 years and made it the wool capital of the Midlands. Coventry merchants became prosperous, not only exporting cloth around the country but also to Flanders in France. This cloth carried a lead seal stamped with an elephant to prove it was true high-quality Coventry cloth and 'that the city may have praise by it and no slander', as it would from the sale of inferior, falsely-named Coventry cloth. Merchants and traders were physically encouraged to settle in Coventry in this early period. Early charters, for their benefit, made the growing town into an early English 'enterprise zone'. The threat of a loss of trade caused by the import of foreign wools was averted in 1337 when Edward III introduced an act which forbade English subjects from wearing anything but English wool. This act ensured the prosperity of English wool towns like Coventry.

The processing and weaving of wool, and the production of cloth, girdles and caps naturally led to the art of dyeing. The dyeing of wool in Coventry was considered a highly specialized craft, and the city grew famous for its beautiful blue dye, made from sloe berries, which never faded and gave rise to the saying 'as true as Coventry blue'.

Coventry blue items were famed for over 300 years despite being more expensive than other dyed goods. In 1581, however, one writer said 'I have heard say that the chiefe trade of Coventry was heretofore in making of blue thredde and then the towne was rich, even in that trade in manner onely, and now our thredde comes all from beyonde the sea. Wherefore that trade of Coventry is dacaied and thereby the town likewise.' But Coventry survived the foreign threat, and true blue thread could still be acquired into the next century.

Weaving in Coventry has lasted in different forms into the twentieth century and its art was vehemently protected. In 1520 it was enacted that 'no person of the craft teach no points of the craft to no person save his apprentice and his wife.' Even into the eighteenth century the art was protected, for in 1780 an apology appeared in the *Coventry Mercury*: 'I William Newey, a worsted weaver, publish an apology for having instructed some Spanish prisoners, resident in this city, the art and mystery of the worsted manufacture.'

The early growth of Coventry brought the order of the Greyfriars (Franciscans) to settle here around 1234. Their church and monastery was built on land given to them by Ranulf, Earl of Chester, before his death in 1232. The Franciscans won favour in the city and many important citizens chose to be buried at their house. (The church spire of the Greyfriars still stands next to the Methodist Central Hall in Greyfriars Lane.)

In the early years of the fourteenth century two incidents happened which threw light upon the minds of our ancestors and their beliefs. The first case concerns Walter Langton, Bishop of Coventry and Lord Treasurer of England. In the year 1301 Langton was accused by Sir John Lovetot of being a sorcerer who had sold his soul to the devil and paid homage to the devil. Lovetot also accused him of murdering his father, for adultery with Lovetot's stepmother, and also various ecclesiastical offences, including the buying and selling of church favours. Despite his denials, Langton was summoned to Rome. Here Pope Boniface VIII kept the disgraced bishop waiting over seven months before ordering him back to England, where he was put on trial before a special commission led by the Archbishop of Canterbury. The bishop called up thirty-seven witnesses to vouch for his innocence and, after a long and difficult trial, he was found not guilty of the charges. Two years had passed, and somehow Langton had to pay back the huge expenses that he had incurred. The trial may have originated in personal malice against the bishop, or Lovetot may have actually believed his accusations. Belief of black magic was a very real thing, as the next case testifies.

The trial in Coventry of John de Nottingham and Robert Mareschal in 1325 is said to be the oldest recorded witchcraft trial in England. It began just before Christmas 1325, when twenty-seven prominent and respectable Coventry citizens visited the house of one John de Nottingham, cleric and practitioner of the black arts, in Shortley (the Charterhouse area) by the London Road. These prominent Coventry men complained of the crushing taxes and rents forced on them by the king and the prior of Coventry. They offered Nottingham £20 and free maintenance in any religious house of his choice, and £15 for his assistant Robert Mareschal, if he would use his magic to destroy the king, prior, Hugh le Despencer, his son the Earl of Winchester, and the seneschal and cellarer of the priory. Nottingham agreed and, after being supplied with four pounds of wax and two lengths of canvas, set about creating wax effigies of the victims. He also made an extra figure, the image of Richard de Sowe who lived nearby (probably in Walsgrave). Sowe's image was to prove the effectiveness of his powers. At midnight on 27 April 1324 Nottingham handed Mareschal a leaden pin and ordered him to thrust it into the head of the image of Richard de Sowe. The following morning Mareschal was sent to check their handiwork and found Richard in a state of lunacy, shouting and screaming and unable to recognize those around him.

These facts were reported back to the men's employers, and for further proof they called for Sowe's death. Ten days later, Nottingham pulled the pin from the image's head and pushed it into the heart. Within seven days Richard de Sowe was dead. The sorcerer's magic was proved, and Mareschal began to get nervous. Unable to contain himself he informed on his master and his employers in the hope of saving his own neck. The Sheriff of Warwickshire ordered that all the accused be arrested, but when this was done, while Nottingham and Mareschal were imprisoned, the worthies were released, bailed by various Coventry and Warwickshire gentlemen on condition they returned when trial was called.

The trial itself took place, probably in Coventry Priory, in 1325. John de Nottingham himself could not give evidence, for he had died while in the custody of Robert of Dumbleton, the Marshall of Coventry. Robert Mareschal gave evidence against the Coventry worthies, who all, not surprisingly, walked free after a jury of gentlemen and knights of Warwickshire found them innocent. Robert Mareschal was thrown back into the city dungeons and never heard of again. Many, no doubt, breathed a sigh of relief.

The great war helm (helmet) of Edward the Black Prince. The cat o' mountain which surmounts the helm became part of the city's civic crest

In 1337 the Manor of Cheylesmore came into the hands of Edward the Black Prince, son of Edward III. It was this association with the prince and his grandmother, Queen Isabella, that caused Coventry to become a royal resort. The city motto *Camera Principis*, meaning the 'Prince's treasure chamber' dates from this period. The wild cat, or cat o' mountain, which appears on the city crest, also originated with the Black Prince, appearing on top of his great war-helm, as does the city's use of the three feathers. He adopted the crest from the brave, blind King John of Bohemia who died during the battle of Crécy, where the prince won his spurs. Late in the sixteenth century a verse (now gone) was painted upon a wall in St Mary's guildhall. It read:

Here dwelt the Black Prince, Edward, so we call
This place, whereto he came, The Prince's Hall;
Who from Bohemia's slaughtered King did rest
The snowy plumes that decked this threatening crest;
A hero great in arms, and not less great
To guard our freedom and enrich our state.
Look how his Arms upon our walls appear,
And learn how still we hold his memory dear.

The first merchant guild, the guild of St Mary, was founded in Coventry in 1340 and held its meetings in the earliest part of St Mary's Hall, in Bayley Lane, built in the 1340s. Over the following years other guilds were founded, these being the guilds of St John, St Catherine, Corpus Christi and Trinity. Three of these four religious mercantile guilds amalgamated (except for Corpus Christi), and became a more powerful single guild, calling itself Trinity Guild. Trinity Guild was responsible for building the present St Mary's Hall around the year 1400. Trinity and Christi guilds dominated the city council, and those in it became some of the most important individuals within the city, and outside. One member was Sir Richard (Dick) Whittington, thrice mayor of London. As the guilds developed they came to be controlled mainly by merchants, so the craftsmen of Coventry began to set up their own craft guilds, which became responsible for the industries in the city. These guilds had amongst them the drapers, dyers, tailors and smiths, for example. Many of these guilds held their own chapels within St Michael's and Holy Trinity churches, and with their patronage the churches grew.

The year 1343 saw the building of Whitefriars, near the London Road. Sir John Poultney, four times Mayor of London, paid for its erection, and the monastery housed fourteen friars of the Carmelite

St Mary's Hall, the guildhall of Coventry, is considered one of the finest of its type in England. Many notable people have visited this fine hall

order. Coventry's prosperity and importance was confirmed on 20 January 1345, as Edward III granted a charter of incorporation to the town. This gave the citizens the right to elect a mayor (the first was John Ward), a council and bailiffs and constituted the first act of incorporation for an English borough. The Prior of Coventry, however, opposed this, as it threatened to put an end to his ecclesiastical control within the city. Little was left from Earl Leofric's charter to the priory. Most manors had been lost, leaving the priory with its land outside the city, on the north (Radford, Coundon, Keresley, Whitemoor, Newland)

and to the east (Sowe, now Walsgrave, Willenhall, Harnall and Hawkesbury). Although losing political power the Priory did, however, retain its now much reduced economic power.

Many of the prior's tenants in those areas died in 1350, when the Black Death swept the land. This epidemic was so deadly that it was said there were scarcely enough living left to bury the dead. The graveyards were soon filled and the dead had to be buried in the fields; even the mayor Jordan Sheppey and William Irreys, the prior, fell to the visitation. The city streets echoed in the night to the chilling cry of 'Bring out your dead', while out in the fields crops spoiled and mill wheels failed to turn, for there was no-one left to serve them.

The following year of 1351 is recorded in the City Annals as being notable for the fact that one morning four suns were seen shining in the sky, until midday when the objects merged into one. This may have been due to some extremely rare weather condition, or maybe it would now be called a UFO sighting. Whatever it was, this aerial phenomenon would have been observed with great fear, for such things were considered omens of impending disaster. Many may have feared that the plague would end the world.

More mundane things were happening, however, for the prior's earlier acquisition of most of the Cheylesmore estate, from Roger de Montalt, and his attempt to split the city by creating his own moot and trade centre was brought to an end by Queen Isabella. Her enforced reclamation ended with the signing of the Tripartite Indenture which united the city, ending the prior's power game. From this time the prior totally relinquished the rights he still held over the city, and gave them to the city corporation.

CHAPTER SIX

Defence and Defiance

When Taylor, 'the water poet', came to Coventry during his summer tour of England in 1639, he described the city as 'a faire famous, sweet, and ancient city, so walled about with such strength and neatnesse as no city in England may compare with it.' What Taylor saw began in January 1329, when Edward III gave the prior and citizens of Coventry the right to the duty on goods over a period of six years, to finance the building of a wall to enclose the city – which had grown so rich and of strategic importance that it needed protection. Despite these early beginnings nothing was done until 1355, when the mayor, Richard Stoke, laid the first stone at New Gate, near Whitefriars on the London Road. The walling of the city then proceeded in a clockwise direction, as the southern half of the city had natural barriers to protect it, such as the Sherbourne, Swanswell, Mill Dam (St Osburg's Pool), the Babba-lacu and probably remains of the Hyrsum Ditch.

The work was very slow moving, for in 1363 Edward the Black Prince granted another licence, 'to enclose the City with a wall of lime and stone, embattailed'. Three years later a new heavier tax against the citizens and traders was levied to finance the building of the wall. Richard II confirmed the previous charters, and gave stone from his quarry at Cheylesmore to erect Greyfriars Gate, and enough wall to encompass the manor house in Cheylesmore. In 1372 he granted stone for the building of Spon Gate, said to have been the finest of the city's twelve gates. The king also gave all the waste ground belonging to him within the city boundaries, so that it could be used to finance the wall. The construction of the wall is said to have ended around 1400, although some have suggested that it lasted until the 1530s. What we do know is that the wall evolved through various stages, with parts being extended and gates and towers added to develop its defensive capability.

When completed, the city wall was an impressive structure measuring nearly 2 1/2 miles round. The wall consisted of two red-sandstone

Spon Gate stood next to St John's church between Spon and Fleet Street. Part of it was recently excavated and its position marked at the entrance to Spon Street

Swanswell Gate, built at the request of the prior in 1461. Now an artist's studio and craft shop the gateway has previously been used as a shop and cottage

walls, infilled with rubble and 9 ft thick, with five main gates where roads entered the city. These were Bishop Gate (which gave access to Bishop Street), Gosford Gate (Gosford Street), New Gate (by Whitefriars, London Road), Greyfriars Gate (Warwick Lane) and Spon Gate (Fleet Street/Spon Street). The minor gates interspersed between the main gates were, Cook Street (or Tower) Gate (Cook Street), Swanswell or Priory Gate (Hales Street), Bastile or Mill Lane Gate (Cox Street), Little Park Gate (Little Park Street), Cheylesmore Gate (Warwick Road), Bablake or Hill Gate (Hill Street) and Well Street Gate (Well Street). Whitefriars Gate, which can be found in Much Park Street, was built in 1352 and formed the west entrance to Whitefriars. Between these twelve city gates could be found between twenty and thirty-two square and round towers, many of which in troubled times bore cannons. It was possible to walk around the outside of the city at between 12 and 15 ft off the ground. Outside the wall was a defensive ditch, which could in times of trouble be flooded.

The citizens of Coventry paid an annual tax called murage (from the Latin *murus*, a wall) for the upkeep and maintenance of the city wall. All Coventry slept safe within the massive walls and when the gates were closed at nine o'clock no one could enter until the ringing of the daybell. In times of trouble the citizens themselves were elected to provide 'watch and ward' around the wall.

One of the most famous of the city wall towers was next to Whitefriars, the Lady Tower. Sir William Dugdale, the Warwickshire antiquarian, wrote of it that 'This Chappell is in y't tower of the Cittye wall without New Gate, close by the roadway leading towards London. On the outside thereof was a picture of the Blessed Virgin richly paynted, and within it an image and her altar.' Travellers passing prayed here, or saluted the image so their journey would be blessed. A nearby inn was called the Salutation because of this. By the reign of Henry VI, visitors came especially to visit Our Lady of the Tower, for the image had gained a reputation of having great protective power.

The first test walled Coventry had was in 1395, when 200 armed men led by William Bagot of Baginton Castle tried to get into the city by attacking two of the gates. Their attempt failed miserably, but left the city more aware of its strategic military importance. The second scare was in 1450, when Jack Cade, a veteran soldier, led risings in Kent and Sussex. Riots ensued in the south, and the city burgesses decided that Coventry could come under threat. Forty armed men were placed on guard walking the wall between sunset and daybreak. Once daytime came the defence of the city lay in the hands of all its citizens, many of whom would not have been unfamiliar with the art of warfare.

Opposite: Cook Street Gate, the exit to the road to Leicester. This early nineteenth-century print shows the ditch outside the gate which formed part of the city's defences

This decision to guard the city was soon proved right, for within a week Cade had beaten the royal army and led an army of 30,000 rebels into London. King Henry VI left the capital and came to the safety of Coventry. Two large serpentine bronze cannon and two smaller cannon were brought to the city from Bristol, and were mounted in Spon Gate, while Spon and New Gate were both portcullised and the wall ditch was scraped out and made ready for flooding, via the Sherbourne. Cade's rebellion soon fell apart as the citizens of London turned against him, because of the outrages of his men. The rebels moved back into Kent and a promised pardon broke up the army. Cade himself was captured and killed.

These threats to the city made it more ready for such incidents: its armoury grew and an alarm system was set up, the ringing of which ensured that all the city's gates would be immediately closed and the walls would be manned.

During the Wars of the Roses, between the houses of Lancaster and York, Coventry held within its wall men from both sides. In the past, the men of Coventry had fought under King Edward IV's Yorkist banner. The king came to the city directly after the battle of Towton, in which Coventry men fought, and afterwards visited the city on several occasions. On one such occasion the Earl of Warwick closed the gates against him (see chapter nine).

The wall once again formed a significant barrier in 1642, when the gates were closed to King Charles I and later his nephew Prince Rupert during the Civil War. (See chapter thirteen.) In 1662, Charles II ordered the city walls breached so they could no longer be used as a stronghold against the monarchy. In accordance with the king's orders, the Earl of Northampton, accompanied by a train of local gentry (former Royalists) and 500 troops came to Coventry, and on 22 July 1662 began to slight the city's ancient wall. The Earl of Northampton symbolically made the first breach at New Gate, where Charles I had been repulsed. The work, which lasted three weeks and cost £500, was said to have far exceeded the king's orders, for the breaching had ended as a near demolition of the walls. Mother Shipton, the fifteenth-century prophetess, is said to have predicted that a pigeon would one day cause the walls of Coventry to fall. In 1662 the mayor of Coventry agreed to the destruction of the walls. His name was Thomas Pidgeon.

Practically all of the city gates seem to have survived this vandalism, and Thomas Sharp's map of 1807 shows large sections of wall running from the London Road to Little Park Street, from modern Manor Road to Warwick Lane, then from the modern Bull Yard to the Sherbourne towards Fleet Street. Then another section runs from Well Street to

Lamb Street, then from the bottom of Leicester Row to Cook Street, down to Swanswell Gate and onwards to the Sherbourne in Lower Cox Street. There was also a short stretch near the present ring road, which can now be seen south of Godiva Street, near Gosford Street. The last two sections on Sharp's map stood between Gosford Street and the bottom of Gulson Road, and by Whitefriars.

Almost all the city gates, despite their antiquity, were demolished. New Gate in 1762; Gosford Gate in 1765; Spon Gate in 1771; Greyfriars Gate in 1781 and Bastille or Mill Gate in 1849. Two gates survived into present times, these being Cook Street Gate, and Swanswell or Priory Gate. These two gates are joined by the longest surviving section of the city wall, which runs through Lady Herbert's Garden. This section was restored and landscaped in 1931–2 and presented to the city by the industrialist Sir Alfred Herbert, as a memorial to his late wife.

Remains of two towers can still be found. One, part of a round tower still with a section of wall, is in an alleyway off Upper Well Street, and the other is near King Street, off St Columba's Close.

Bastille Gate at the bottom of Cox Street was demolished in 1849, the last city gate to suffer such a fate

34

CHAPTER SEVEN

Mystery Plays and Mortal Combat

A fter half the population had been wiped out by the Black Death, agricultural labourers sought higher wages for their more valuable labour. The Government and landowners, however, tried to keep wages down, which brought much discontent to the kingdom. This discontent turned to full rebellion when a poll-tax of 1s per head was placed on the population. John Ball, a priest, stirred the rebellion in 1381, becoming one of its leaders. His speech on Blackheath ended with the words:

> When Adam delved and Eve span,
> Who was then the gentleman?

These words were meant to stir class hatred and they did; a peasant army of 100,000 marched on London, leaving slaughtered officials in its wake. Fourteen-year-old King Richard II faced the army with the Mayor of London at Mile End, sending many on their way with unfulfillable promises. Wat Tyler, the insurgent leader from Kent, stayed, and during a later meeting with the king was struck down dead by the mayor, an act which brought the rebellion to an end. Hearing the news, Ball fled to Coventry and hid in the house of relatives or friends until he was finally captured and executed.

During these troubled times building work was being carried out. Holy Trinity was extended and the building of St Michael's tower (begun in 1373) was well under way. William and Adam Botoner, wealthy merchants, paid for the erection of the tower, at a cost of £100 a year for twenty-two years. Their sisters Ann and Mary then paid for the spire, beginning in 1432, and also claimed to have paid for the church and choir. Coventry's population was now estimated at 9,000.

Richard II came to Coventry on the Feast of Corpus Christi (18 June) in 1384. During his stay at the priory he witnessed the mystery plays and laid the foundation stone of the Carthusian Charterhouse on the London Road, dedicating it to St Anne.

Coventry was one of England's famed centres for the production of pageants or mystery plays. The plays had their origin in church dramas, but were at some point taken over by the people and played in the streets at the feast of Corpus Christi. Coventry's craft guilds had control of the plays by the mid-fourteenth century, and a document exists from 1392 stating that the Drapers' Guild stored its props in a 'pageant house' in Little Park Street.

The pageants began at five in the morning, with a procession followed by each city guild recreating stories from the Bible, from the Creation to Domesday. The plays were acted out on portable stages, or pageants, which were wheeled to different parts of the city: Gosford Street, Much Park Street corner, New Gate, Broadgate, Cross Cheaping, Greyfriars Gate, Spon Gate and Bishop Gate. The decorative wagons were two-storied and canopied, with the lower section curtained off and used by the players as a dressing room. The upper section formed the stage and was decorated with simple props. The last play of the pageant was often reached at nightfall. This was Domesday, in which a monstrous head called Hell's Mouth spat smoke and flames. Occasionally the devil himself appeared and dragged a victim into hell, amid the roars of the crowd. In these last scenes the drapers set fire to a paper image of the world, symbolizing the end.

The man who played Herod in the pageants almost became a comic character, running around the stage and among the crowds, raging like a madman. The day of the pageant saw the streets packed with people, for afterwards the fair was held. Visitors came from miles around, including no doubt the young Will Shakespeare, who may have got his early taste for the theatre from the pageants. Shakespeare's later reference to 'it out-Herods Herod' probably refers to his memory of the ragings of Herod in the Coventry mystery plays.

The last performance of the mystery plays was in 1589. Religious ideals were changing, and the old plays smacked of popery in antipapist Protestant England. The plays were sorely missed by the people, and by the traders who benefited through the increase in trade they brought. In 1584 the guilds enacted *The Destruction of Jerusalem*, a Protestant play written by John Smythe of Oxford. It was a failure, but despite this it was ordered by the city leet to be played again in 1591. On this second performance the Smiths Guild paid 20s to excuse them

An act of the mystery play cycle underway just inside Spon Street. In the background can be seen Spon Gate

from taking part. This was the end of the united guild pageants, for Smythe's play could not replace the ancient mystery plays or the excitement, wonder and fun they evoked.

Apart from the modern re-enactment of the plays in the cathedral ruins, nothing has survived into the twentieth century of the pageants, except a song, better known today as the Coventry Carol. This hauntingly beautiful song was probably first sung over 550 years ago, during the Tailors' and Shearmans' pageant, The Birth of Christ, and was movingly performed among the ruins of Coventry Cathedral, after its destruction in 1940.

Richard II witnessed the mystery plays here and also laid the foundation stone of the Charterhouse on the London Road

* * *

John Onley, the mayor in 1396, is recorded as being the first Englishman born in Calais, after its capture by Edward III in 1347. John's father, a Coventrian, was standard bearer to the king. Before coming to Coventry John Onley was twice Mayor of Calais. Thomas Mowbray was the Constable of Calais Castle and was thought to have been the king's agent in the murder of the Duke of Gloucester at the castle in 1397. Whereas John Onley came to the city to take up a civic role, Thomas Mowbray was 'sent to Coventry' by the king for reasons entirely different.

For his service to Richard II, Mowbray was awarded the title of Duke of Norfolk. Henry Bolingbroke, another noble of great popularity, was elevated about the same time, becoming the Duke of Hereford. The dukes disliked each other and vied for royal favour. Soon they quarrelled, and Norfolk accused Hereford of muttering treasonable words against the king. In January 1398 Norfolk made the charge openly before Parliament, and Hereford swore the charges were untrue. As no court could settle the charge the king stepped in and declared that the two dukes settle their argument with trial by combat. Richard called for the combat to take place on St Lambert's day (17 September) on Gosford Green, Coventry.

Great preparations were made for the event and Coventry soon found itself flooded with people. Shakespeare wrote of this famed event in *Richard II*, while another version of events is given by the chronicler Raphael Holinshead. The last moments of the joust read as follows:

The Duke of Hereford was quickly horsed and closed his beaver [visor], and cast his spear into the rest and when the trumpet sounded, set forward courageously towards his enemy six or seven paces.

Richard II calls a halt to the duel. Little did he know that the outcome of these events would end his life. His next visit to Coventry would be as a prisoner

The Duke of Norfolk was not fully set forward, when the king cast down his warder [a short sceptre] and the heralds cried, 'Ho, ho'. Then the king caused their spears to be taken from them, and commanded them to return again to their chairs, where they remained two long hours while the king and his council deliberately consulted what order was best to be had in so weighty a cause.

The heralds called for silence and Sir John Bushy proclaimed the decision of the king and council. He said that 'Henry, Duke of Hereford, should within fifteen days depart out of the realm and not return before the term of ten years were expired, except he should be recalled again by the king; and this upon pain of Death. Also that Thomas Mowbray, Duke of Norfolk, because he had sown sedition in the realm by his words, should likewise leave the realm and never return again into England, nor approach the borders or confines thereof, upon pain of death.'

The two would-be combatants then swore not to pursue their quarrel abroad:

The Duke of Norfolk departed sorrowfully out of the realm into Almaine, and at last came to Venice, where he died of brooding and melancholy; for he was in hope that he should have been borne out of the matter by the king. The Duke of Hereford took his leave of the king at Eltham, who there released four years of his banishment; so he took his journey over into Calais, and from thence went into France, where he remained.

In 1399 the exiled Henry Bolingbroke, Duke of Hereford, returned to England, gathered an army and took Richard prisoner. It was as a prisoner that the king was next brought to Coventry; here he was held before being taken to London, where he was forced to abdicate the crown to his one-time favourite. Henry Bolingbroke, a descendant of Edward, was crowned Henry IV and ruled until 1413. As for Richard, he was murdered by Henry's order in 1400.

Richard's decision on Gosford Green changed the course of history, for if he had not exiled two of his most favoured dukes, the Lancastrian kings would never have sat on the throne of England and the War of the Roses would never have happened. Richard would have ruled for the rest of his natural life, thus changing the history of our royal family.

CHAPTER EIGHT

Coventry, England's Other Capital

The acquisition of the crown by the Lancastrians began a succession of royal visits to the city. Henry IV needed money to fight rebellion, and cities such as Coventry lent it to him. Henry came to Coventry fresh from his victory over Henry 'Hotspur' Percy at the battle of Shrewsbury.

Here in 1404 Henry summoned Parliament. Having found lawyers particularly troublesome in previous parliaments, Henry called for none to be present: for this reason the Parliament was called the 'Parliament Indoctorum' or the 'Unlearned Parliament'. Hundreds of knights, nobles and clergy entered the city, taking lodgings wherever they could.

Parliament met within the great hall of the Priory. The king needed more money but, not wanting to impose more taxes, the knights, nobles and burgesses suggested that the king raised more money from the Church. 'The knights complained that, while they were constantly taking the field against rebels or foreign foes, and not merely contributing money, but perilling their own bodies, the clergy sat safe and quiet at home helping the King in no ways.' The Archbishop of Canterbury defended the church, saying its help was of a spiritual nature. Sir John Cheyne, Speaker of the House of Commons, said that he put no value on prayer, and that money was more use in war. The Parliament argued for over a month, but finally the Church kept its revenue and Parliament gave in, granting the king money.

Tradition tells us that in 1411 the Prince of Wales (later Henry V) was arrested by Mayor John Horneby in the Priory. This, like the many stories of the Prince's wild youth, is thought by many to be untrue. Shakespeare in his *Henry V* tells of Prince Hal meeting Sir John Falstaff on the road to Coventry. Falstaff, legend states, was born in Coventry and spent his youth at Caludon Castle. Being a companion of the prince and a noted drinker, maybe the arrest of a drunken prince in the priory is not that far from the truth.

Four years after this event, Henry V was in France to claim the throne from Charles VI. At Agincourt, on St Crispin's Day, Henry and his army of 5,000 faced an overwhelming force of over 15,000 French knights and slaughtered 10,000 of them. The English army lost 1,500 men, giving them France and victory. Thereafter, 'Harry of England' was a national hero.

Henry VI was a regular visitor to Coventry. He gave the city the status of county which it retained until 1842

In 1421 Henry came to Coventry with his French queen, Catherine. Both were presented with 100 marks and a traditional gift, a gold cup. The following year Catherine found herself a widow with a nine-month-old child. The baby was crowned King Henry VI, and two months later King of France. Henry VI visited Coventry in 1436, and the following year was declared of age to run the country. He married Margaret of Anjou in 1445, when he was twenty-four. The marriage involved the signing of a secret treaty by Henry which gave Maine back to France. On hearing this the English nobles were furious. Coventry supported Henry in 1448, when England was at war, not only with France but also Scotland. Coventry men fought under the banner of the black ram, because of the wool trade. In 1448 twenty-three city companies armed 600 Coventry men to fight for the king in France and Scotland.

On 22 September 1451 Henry paid a state visit to Coventry, approaching the city via the Radford Road and Bishop Street. He was met at Radford Hazelwood, 'beyond the Broad-oak', by Richard Boys, the mayor, dressed in scarlet, and the Commonalty, clad in green gowns and red hoods, all on horseback. They dismounted and kneeled before the king, the mayor greeting him with these words: 'Most highest and gracious King, you are welcome to your true liege men, with all our hearts.' After some further ceremony the cavalcade moved on through Bishop Gate towards the priory. The procession was led by the bailiffs.

The king stayed at the priory for ten days, until the Tuesday after Michaelmas. On the eve of Michaelmas Henry mentioned his intention to hear high mass at St Michael's church on the following day, and commanded the attendance of the mayor and his peers. On the morning of Michaelmas Day a procession walked from the priory, entered by the great west door, and took the king to a reserved place where he could join in the service uninterrupted. When the service was over, the procession returned. After Evensong the king gave the sable gown which he had worn that morning for the use of St Michael's church.

Before he left, Henry repaid Coventry's loyalty to him by conferring on it the status of county, within itself. Making up the County of

Opposite: St Michael's was the largest parish church in England until it became a cathedral in 1918. Its tower and spire are the third tallest in England, measuring nearly 300 ft

Coventry were the villages of Whoberley, Biggin, Stoke, Wyken, Caludon, part of Walsgrave (then Sowe), Ansty, Radford, Keresley, Harnell, Foleshill, Pinley, Whitley, Styvechale, Exhall, Wood End, Asthull and Horwell, covering an area of around 20 square miles. As a county, Coventry became responsible for its own assize and gaol, and remained separate from Warwickshire until 1842.

The mayor and commonalty rode with the king for Kenilworth, until they came to 'a piece beyond Astill Grove'. The king gave his leave, and declared that thereafter the bailiffs of the city should become sheriffs, officers to the king. Henry then left, thanking the mayor and commonalty for their 'good rule' once again.

Henry and Queen Margaret came back to Coventry in 1453, and stayed at the priory. A short time afterwards the queen gave birth to Edward, and Henry's mind became unhinged with madness, probably inherited from his grandfather, Charles VI of France. France itself was lost and unruly bands of soldiers began to return to England. Richard, Duke of York was proclaimed regent and Edmund Beaufort, Duke of Somerset, was blamed for the defeats in France and thrown into the Tower.

Suddenly in 1454 Henry recovered; York was dismissed and Somerset was released. York, however, although not openly claiming the crown, raised an army. Henry was taken prisoner and York was proclaimed lord protector. In 1456 Margaret was back in Coventry. She was welcomed at Bablake (Spon) Gate by a pageant all the way to Broadgate, and the city conduits ran with wine. A council was held in the city and the Duke of York, fearing an attempt on his life, fled.

The king and queen were again in Coventry the following year, 'that the king might enjoy the sports of the field', and another council was held, this time in an attempt to reconcile York with the monarchs, thus healing the rift between the houses of Lancaster and York. On Corpus Christi Day in 1458 the queen came from Kenilworth to watch the mystery plays. She stayed at the house of Richard Wood, a grocer of some means. The city provided huge quantities of food, including 120 gallons of wine. These constant visits gained Coventry the nickname of 'Queen Margaret's secret arbour'.

In 1459 the Wars of the Roses began in earnest. After the Yorkist victory at Bloreheath, the Yorkist army marched north and was joined by Richard Neville, Earl of Warwick. Queen Margaret collected the Lancastrian forces together at Coventry and pursued the Yorkists – who were vastly outnumbered and fled. The Duke of York fled to Ireland, and the Earls of Salisbury and Warwick, with the duke's son, the Earl of March, fled to Calais. The king and queen returned to

Coventry and once again summoned Parliament. Coventry was becoming the second capital of England. This Parliament, made up entirely of Lancastrians, met in the chapter house of the priory on 20 November 1459. Sitting for over a month, it condemned the Duke of York and his supporters to death for treason. This Parliament, called the *Parliamentum Diabolicum,* put an end to any chance of a reconciliation between the two houses.

In June 1460, while Henry and Margaret were again in Coventry, they received news that the Earls of Salisbury, Warwick and March had landed with foreign troops. Margaret marched south and was outmanoeuvred and defeated by the Yorkists. Henry was taken, and Margaret fled north, while York returned from Ireland and claimed the throne of England. Parliament reversed the condemnation order against York, and Henry agreed that York should become Lord Protector, proclaiming him his heir. Meanwhile Margaret collected an army in the north.

The Duke of York marched north to check the threat, but at Wakefield he was forced into battle and slain. Salisbury was captured and executed. Lord Clifford presented York's head to Margaret, decorated with a paper crown, and she ordered it and Salisbury's head to be put on display in York.

After York's death the Earl of Warwick successfully dominated the war, and Coventry decided to change sides. A contingent of men was sent to join the Yorkist army as it headed for London. After vicious and bloody battles, with Henry's escape and recapture, and the proclamation of Edward of York, Earl of March as King Edward IV in 1461 Edward sent a letter to the mayor and citizens of Coventry thanking them for their 'good and substantial rule', and for keeping the city at peace during the time of conflict. The peace, however, was not permanent.

CHAPTER NINE

The End of the War

C hristmas 1465 saw Edward and his new bride, Elizabeth Woodville, staying at Coventry Priory. During this time of feasting and celebration the king probably gave the city the royal privilege to strike his new 'light coinage'. These coins, bearing the 'C' for Coventry, consisted of gold ryals, half-ryals, silver groats and half-groats. Edward conferred honours on the Woodvilles making the queen's father, Anthony Woodville, Lord Rivers and lord treasurer. Honours and favouritism towards the rest of the Woodvilles who had been Lancastrians caused great offence to the Yorkist nobles of Edward's court. Warwick was sent to the court of France on false negotiations and, furious at this and

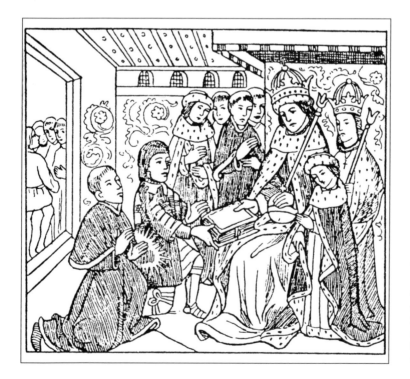

The queen's father, Earl Rivers, presenting Caxton's first book to his daughter and King Edward IV. The unfortunate earl was beheaded on Coventry's Gosford Green

Edward IV came to Coventry first as an honoured guest, later as a prisoner and finally at the head of an army

his ever diminishing power over the king, he began to plot with the king's brother, the Duke of Clarence, to gain overall power in England.

In 1469 rebels from Yorkshire, whose rising had been instigated by Warwick, defeated part of the king's army at Edgecote in Oxfordshire. These rebels brought the queen's father, the Earl Rivers and her brother, the Duke of Norfolk, to Coventry, and beheaded them on Gosford Green.

Warwick and Clarence joined the king in his march north to crush the rebels. Suddenly Edward found himself taken prisoner, brought south to Coventry, then to Warwick Castle, the earl's seat. Once willing to toe the line the king was released. All was quiet for six months until a Lancastrian rising broke out in Lincolnshire. Edward led a force north, and defeated the rebels at Lose-coat Field. Edward returned to London, picking up forty troops as he passed through Coventry. In September, Warwick and Clarence with Jasper Tudor (who had earlier assisted Margaret's attempts to hold the throne) landed in England with French troops, Warwick having fled the country after Lose-Coat Field, where some rebels had admitted being his men.

Releasing Henry VI from the Tower and proclaiming him king, Warwick led his army of 30,000 north, passing through Coventry. The king fled to Flanders, unable to do battle.

In March 1471 Edward landed with 2,000 Burgundians and marched towards London, gathering forces on the way. In Coventry the Earl of Warwick lay with his ordnance and men, waiting for the Duke of Clarence. Edward spent the night at Coombe Abbey, and the following day headed for Coventry intending to pick up troops. Sending knights forward to announce his approach the king was shocked to find Gosford Gate closed against him. Demands for entrance fell on deaf ears. The king was not in a position to place Coventry under siege, so chose to leave and headed for Warwick. As he left his brother, the Duke of Clarence, arrived and promptly changed sides, for if Henry held the throne he could never succeed to it. A day later Warwick rode after the king, who entered London throwing Henry once again into the Tower. Edward, together with the Dukes of Clarence and Gloucester, headed back north to face Warwick at Barnet, Hertfordshire where the 'Kingmaker' was finally cut down by knights.

Margaret having landed at Weymouth with Prince Edward, and the Dukes of Somerset and Beaufort, and the Tudors raising a force in Wales, the king marched south to stop the two forces meeting. Battle was fought at Tewkesbury on 4 May, and Margaret's army was totally

A mid-nineteenth century engraving of Gosford Gate. Here Edward demanded entrance and was refused by the Earl of Warwick

defeated. Prince Edward was killed. Margaret escaped, but was captured two days later and thrown in the Tower. On the same night it is said that Henry VI was murdered in the Tower by the Duke of Gloucester.

Before King Edward returned to London he came to Coventry and for its disloyalty deprived the mayor, John Betts, of his sword (a symbol of the monarch's favour) and the city of its privileges. The fall from grace only lasted a short period, for the king accepted 500 marks for the restoration of rights. This was due to the Duke of Clarence who pleaded on Coventry's behalf, on a promise that the city would return

A silver Coventry Groat, now a rare collector's item. This and other gold coins were struck, tradition states, in the mint on the site of the Golden Cross Inn

A Victorian engraving of Henry VII. He visited Coventry directly after the battle of Bosworth and he and Queen Margaret became regular visitors to the city

a jewelled coronal he had pawned to it some years earlier. One royal privilege which seems not to have been returned was the right to strike coins, for no Coventry coins seem to have been struck in or after 1471.

The battle of Tewkesbury and the following executions stirred a rising in Kent and, as they had in 1381, the Kentish rebels marched on London, burnt London Bridge and camped on Blackheath. This rebellion was quickly crushed, and its leaders were sent to Coventry to be hanged, drawn and quartered, probably in Broadgate or at the Conduit in Smithford Street.

In April 1474 Edward the Prince of Wales came to the city to celebrate the Feast of St George. He was met at the Grove at Syvechale by the mayor and commons dressed in 'Grene and Blewe'. Being then only three years old, the prince was seated in a chair strapped to a horse. He was entertained as he entered the city by various characters: 'Upon the Conduit in Cross Cheaping, was Saint George armed, and a king's daughter kneeling before him with a lamb; and the father and mother being in a tower, above, beholding, St George saving their daughter from the dragon; and the conduit running wine in four places, and minstrels playing organs.'

The young prince was presented with a gold cup containing 100 marks, was admitted to the guilds, and made godfather to the mayor's son. Three years later the prince returned and stayed at Cheylesmore Manor. It is said that over the following years the prince was a regular visitor there, until his death in the Tower with his brother, while under the 'safekeeping' of their uncle Richard, Duke of Gloucester, later Richard III. Coventry's close association with the princes of Wales seems to end at this point.

The year 1478 is notable for the fact that out of the city's population of about 9,000, 3,300 people died of the plague in Coventry and its county villages. This decline in population reflected Coventry's general commercial decline, and the falling quality of its wool and cloth.

Richard III visited in 1484 to see the pageants, while he stayed at nearby Kenilworth Castle. The following year the ill-fated monarch faced the army of Henry Tudor, Duke of Richmond, at Bosworth in Leicestershire. Here Richard perished, and his naked body was slung over a horse's back and put on display in Leicester. His crown was recovered from a bush and taken by Lord Stanley, who crowned Henry Tudor on the battlefield, proclaiming him Henry VII. The Wars of the Roses had finally ended.

The newly proclaimed Welsh Tudor king came straight to Coventry, and stayed at the house of the mayor, Robert Onley, next to the Bull Conduit in Smithford Street. Onley sat the monarch down to a feast

This fifteenth-century illustration showing an execution could easily have been based on the beheading of the pretender Thomas Harrington in Smithford Street

which consisted of, among other things, twenty sheep, two oxen, 240 gallons of wine and hundreds of gallons of ale. After the feast Henry was presented with the customary gold cup and £100; he returned the compliment by making the mayor Sir Robert Onley.

Two years later, in 1487, a number of pretenders tried to lay claim to the throne. Henry returned to Coventry, once again staying with Sir Robert. Here an army was raised that on 10 June fought the battle of Stoke in which a certain Thomas Harrington, who claimed to be the son of the Duke of Clarence and therefore in direct line to the throne, was captured. The pretender was sent to Coventry to await the king's pleasure. Henry arrived at Sir Robert's house before Corpus Christi and watched the mystery plays. On the Wednesday after St Peter's Day (29 June) Henry watched from the mayor's house as Thomas Harrington was beheaded on the Bull Conduit next door (now the site of Marks & Spencer). The remains of the pretender were then interred at Greyfriars graveyard (site of the Methodist Central Hall).

Henry VII and his queen, Elizabeth of York, became regular visitors to Coventry. In 1492, for example, they came to witness the mystery plays. The king once again used the city as a place of execution in 1495, when Sir Henry Mumford and Sir Robert Mallory were sent to Coventry to be executed for treason. The beheading took place under Binley Gallows, which stood on the site of the Craven Arms on the Binley Road. Mumford's head was placed on a pole on Bablake Gate and Mallory's head on Bishop Gate, and their bodies were buried at Greyfriars. When Shelton excavated the proposed site of Central Hall he unearthed a large number of skeletons, which were re-interred behind the hall. Two skulls were found, buried in clay, and are thought to be those of Mallory and Mumford.

The twelve-year-old Prince of Wales, Arthur, visited in 1497 and received the usual gift. Arthur married Catherine of Aragon, who received as part of her dowry Cheylesmore Manor and certain ground rents in the city. Arthur died six months after the marriage, aged sixteen. In 1499 Henry and Elizabeth returned and received the distinction (as did Henry VI and Margaret) of becoming brother and sister to (special members of) the powerful Trinity Guild. Henry VII died in 1509, leaving the throne to his son, Henry VIII, who would physically alter the city for ever.

CHAPTER TEN

Religious Upheavals and Martyrs

H enry VIII inherited a rich kingdom, due to his father's financial acumen. There was, however, religious unrest in England: the Church was losing its grip and many thought that the Latin Bible should be available to all in English. Henry married his brother's widow, Catherine of Aragon, in 1509, and the following year brought her to Coventry.

They stayed in great state at the Priory, which no doubt impressed the young king who would later be responsible for its destruction. Like many previous monarchs they came to witness the mystery plays; this they did from specially constructed, brightly decorated scaffolds. Henry and Catherine watched a pageant by the corner of Much Park Street, featuring 'nine orders of angels'. Then in Broadgate they watched a pageant with 'diverse beautiful damsels' and finally they viewed a pageant in Cross Cheaping. This was Henry's only visit to Coventry, but he was never unaware of its importance to him financially, for he often borrowed from the city. Coventry also supplied men for the army, possibly condemned prisoners; 100 in 1512.

Coventry was suffering from religious upheavals, the seeds of which were sown as far back as the 1380s. It began when John Wycliffe tried to break the hold of the Church by publishing the Bible in English. He was vicar of Lutterworth and converted many to his way of thinking. Many people in Coventry became Lollards, as Wycliffe's followers were known. One man who helped with Wycliffe's Bible was Nicholas Hereford, who was imprisoned until he recanted. He rose to high office in the church, spending his last days, till 1417, living at Coventry's Charterhouse.

John Grace, a Lollard, visited in 1424. He preached to thousands in the Great Park for five days, much to the annoyance of the established clergy. Using the excuse that he had no licence to preach, the prior and

Henry VIII came to Coventry with Queen Catherine in 1509. The destruction of the great priory church was a result of his split with Rome

A nineteenth-century drawing showing how Coventry market may have looked in the sixteenth century. The area in front of the gatehouse was used for baiting bulls

Friar Bredon of Greyfriars tried to have him removed. Violent threats from the people, however, sent both prior and friar to lock themselves in their own houses. These threats reached the king, who sent the Earl of Warwick to Coventry to arrest Grace.

The seeds of Lollardism came to terrible fruition in Henry VIII's and later in Mary's reign. In 1510 several people accused of heresy were forced to carry heavy bundles of faggots (the means of their own death by fire) up and down the market-place in Cross Cheaping before the assembled crowd. One by one they recanted, except for Joan Ward who was condemned to be burnt at the stake in the Little Park.

In 1519 the Bishop of Coventry condemned Mrs Smith, Thomas Lansdail, her brother-in-law, a hosier, Hawkins, a skinner, Wrigsham, a glover, Robert Hockett and Thomas Bond, shoemakers, and Robert Silksby. All except Mrs Smith were found guilty of being heretics. They were condemned to be burnt in the Little Park.

Widow Smith was discharged and Robert Silksby managed to escape. Unfortunately the widow was stopped and searched as she walked home, and was found to be carrying a copy of the Ten Commandments and the Lord's Prayer in English. She was re-arrested and condemned to join the others. Two years later Robert Silksby was recaptured and went to the flaming pit called the 'Park

Hollows'.

In 1527 Henry applied to the Pope to annul his marriage to Catherine as she had borne a daughter, Mary, and was now barren. The Pope refused the request and Henry decided to split from the Church of Rome. By act of Parliament Henry made himself head of the Church of England and the Reformation began. The Church declared his marriage null and void and Roland Lee, Bishop of Coventry and Lichfield, married the king to Anne Boleyn, the Pope excommunicated Henry, and within months Anne gave birth to Elizabeth. Coventry was in favour of reformation as it would end the city's domination by religious houses.

Henry died in 1547 and was succeeded by nine-year-old Edward VI; but England was under the control of his uncle the Duke of Somerset. Under Protestant Somerset religious images and altars were taken from churches and destroyed, and the English prayer book was made compulsory. Edward died aged sixteen and Lady Jane Grey was proclaimed queen in London, but the next day the Mayor of Coventry proclaimed Mary queen. Jane reigned for nine days before she was deposed, and 'Bloody Mary' was crowned. Mary's nickname was well earned, for she began her reign by executing Jane and her husband. She then tried to bring England back to Rome, and within five years 300 Protestants had been put to death.

Coventry witnessed this persecution at first hand with the burning of Laurence Saunders in 1555. He was educated at Cambridge, and after venturing into the commercial world returned there. Saunders was later made rector of All Hallows in London. He married a Coventry woman, and regularly visited and lived in the city during the early years of his marriage.

On the accession of Mary, Saunders preached a Protestant sermon despite a royal proclamation against it. When he was about to deliver his afternoon sermon he was arrested, questioned and thrown into prison. There he remained for fifteen months before being interrogated by the Bishop of London, who asked why Saunders presumed to disregard the queen's command. Saunders replied that he had not called people to hear his words, but simply gave a sermon as normal. He admitted he had broken the royal command, and thought that his long confinement was punishment enough for such an offence.

Saunders was then questioned by the Bishop of Winchester and was offered the chance to turn to the Catholic Church. Saunders's reply was considered unsatisfactory, and Bishop Bonner produced a document against the Catholic Church alleging it was written by Saunders. He was then declared a heretic and sentenced to be sent to Coventry, and burnt at the stake. Coventry was chosen for two reasons: Saunders was known in the city, and Coventry had many Protestants and it was hoped that his death would help to check the growth of this belief.

John Fox, a contemporary of Saunders, wrote:

He was put in the common gaol among other prisoners, where he slept little, but spent the night in prayer and in instructing the others. On the following day, 8 February (1555), he was led to the place of execution in the Park without the city, going in an old gown and a shirt, barefooted, and oftentimes he fell flat on the ground and prayed. When he was come nigh to the place, the officer appointed to see the execution done said to Mr Saunders that he was one of them that corrupted the Queen's realm with false doctrine and heresy; for which, saith he, thou hast deserved death; but yet, if thou wilt revoke thine heresies the Queen will pardon thee; if not yonder fire is prepared for thee. To whom Mr Saunders answered, 'It is not I, nor my fellow preachers of God's truth, that have hurt the Queen's realm; but it is yourself, and such as you are, which have always resisted God's holy word; it is you which have and do corrupt the Queen's realm. I do not hold no heresies, but the doctrine of God, the blessed Gospel of Christ; that hold I, that believe I, and that I will never revoke.' With this the tormentor cried, 'Away with him.' And away from him Mr Saunders went with a merry courage towards the fire. He fell to the ground and prayed. He rose up again,

The results of religious persecution in Coventry. Laurence Saunders was burnt at the stake in the Little Park at the end of Little Park Street

and took the stake to which he should be chained in his arms, and kissed it, saying, 'Welcome, cross of Christ, welcome everlasting life,' and being fastened to the stake, and the fire put to him, full sweetly he slept in the Lord.

The next to suffer was Robert Glover, another learned man, educated at Eton and Oxford, where he gained an MA. In the early part of September 1555 the Privy Council ordered the Mayor of Coventry to arrest John Glover of the Manor House, Mancetter, on suspicion of heresy. Before executing the order Mayor Thomas Ryley sent a man to warn Glover, and he fled. When the officers arrived at the Manor House they found Glover's brother Robert sick in bed, but despite his illness they arrested him and brought him to Coventry.

Robert Glover was taken before Richard Hopkins, city sheriff, who questioned the right of the bishop's men to take him, as his name was not on the warrant. Hopkins wished to release him, but was forced to commit him to the city gaol as he was already under close scrutiny for refusing to torture Laurence Saunders. After eleven days the Bishop of Coventry and Lichfield arrived to hold his inquisition. The bishop questioned Glover's doctrine and asked why he did not attend church. Glover replied that this was because mass was held there. The following day he was told to prepare to leave for Lichfield, together with Cornelius Bongey, a Coventry cooper. Fearing the journey would wreak havoc on his sick body, Glover asked the mayor if he could stay, but the mayor was unable to change the bishop's orders.

Robert Glover told Fox what happened next:

Certain sergeants and constables of Coventry appointed to have the conveying of us to Lichfield, to be delivered to one Jephcot, the Chancellor's man, sent from Coventry with us for the same purpose, (he having come) we were commanded to be on horseback about eleven or twelve of the clock, on Friday, being market day, that we might be more gazed at. . . . He put me in prison that same night, where I continued until I was condemned, in a place next to the dungeon, which was a small room, very cold with little light; and there they allowed me a bundle of hay instead of my bed.

Glover was visited by clergymen who argued with him about his faith. As they failed to make him recant he was condemned to return to Coventry and be burnt. He was brought back to the gaol and there awaited his fate, spending the night in prayer asking for strength to face the ordeal. The following day when he came within sight of the stake in Little Park, he suddenly clapped his hands, saying, 'He is come, He is come,' and went to his fate with joy. Accompanying Robert Glover to his death was Cornelius Bongey, who was sent to the stake for 'holding, maintaining, arguing and teaching' certain doctrines in Coventry and Lichfield that were considered by the sovereign to be heretical.

Two Coventry men who suffered for their beliefs elsewhere were John Careless and Jocelyn Palmer. Careless was a weaver, described by his examiner as 'one of the pleasantest Protestants I have ever met', who died in prison in July 1556. Palmer, whose father was Mayor of Coventry, was a Catholic until he saw Ridley and Latimer burnt at the stake. This led to his own execution by fire in July 1557.

Coventry's sympathetic sheriff, Richard Hopkins, was imprisoned in London for his compassion. On his release the good sheriff was driven into exile until Mary's death, when he returned home.

The site of these barbaric executions lay outside the city wall at the bottom of Little Park Street. The area known as the Park Hollows lay south-east of the memorial. The Hollows, which formed a natural amphitheatre, was the remains of a shallow quarry cut for the city walls, under Richard II's grant of 1385. The area which became known as the Martyrs Field is now covered by the factories between Mile Lane and Parkside. In about 1854, Mr William Mansfield, Keeper of Quinton Park, made a discovery in the Martyrs Field: 'I was digging in the Park Hollows; and when I had dug down about six feet from the surface I came to some very black soil, altogether different from that which I had dug through. I also found some charred or burnt wood, some cinders, and pieces of bright coal. I also found a number of bones, and a piece of silk, which might have been part of a dress, close by the bones.'

The era of religious intolerance ended with the death of 'Bloody Mary'. Upon the ascent of Elizabeth I Catholicism, although not encouraged, was not put down as Protestantism had been. Coventry itself began to move more towards Puritanism.

CHAPTER ELEVEN

Into the Age of Elizabeth

I n December 1541 Sir William Hollis, former Mayor of London and son of Thomas Hollis of Stoke, left £200 in his will to erect a new cross in the market-place in Cross Cheaping, as a lasting memorial of his association with the city. Work began on the cross in 1541 using stone from the quarries at Attleborough and Rowington. The steps, however, needed to be more hard-wearing, and the stone for these was found among the ruins of the old priory.

Coventry Cross was completed in 1543 and exceeded all expectations, becoming one of the most renowned crosses in England. Eventually reaching a height of 57 ft, the Gothic cross was hexagonal, rising in three stages from the base, and topped with an elaborate lantern. The cross had twenty niches in which various figures were carved. In the lower section could be found images of Henry VI (now in St Mary's Hall), King John, Edward I, Henry II (now in Whitefriars), Richard I and Henry V. In the middle section were Edward III, St Michael, Henry II, St George and Richard III. The top section held St Peter, St James, St Christopher and two monks. Some of these figures were taken from the remains of Coventry's dissolved monasteries. At the top of the cross the lantern held figures such as liberty and justice.

Sir William Dugdale the historian of Warwickshire (educated at Coventry grammar school) visited the City to view the cross, and described it as 'one of the chief things wherein this city most glories, which for workmanship and beauty is inferior to none in England.' By 1669 this magnificent edifice was showing its age, and restoration work costing £300 began on it, with £68 being spent on gold leaf. The edifice was ornamented even more, painted in bright new colours and covered in gold. It was said that when the sun shone people were hardly able to look at the glowing cross and horses shied from its brilliance.

Coventry Cross graced Cross Cheaping until 1771, when in a dilapidated condition it was taken down and carted away. Many pieces

Opposite: Coventry Cross in the early eighteenth century: one of the wonders of Coventry. Painted and gilded with gold it shimmered in the sunlight

found their way into city gardens, while other pieces ended up at Keresley House and the Image House in Berkswell.

In the sixteenth century Coventry sat safely within its strong walls. The monastic houses were now gone, turned into quarries, private houses and in one case a pigsty, and the city consisted mainly of ancient timber houses. To lessen the risk of fire, attached houses were tiled, and thatch was only allowed where a house was separate from others. Weekly beast and food markets were held, and Coventry Fair was held every year. Coventry true blue thread was still a major part of the dyeing industry, although the wool and cloth trade were generally in decline. The city's tradesmen still produced caps, gloves, and a variety of fine decorated leather goods. Metalworking was still carried on as it had been since medieval times, but the production had moved on from pins, brooches and buckles to the production of larger-scale decorative and domestic items, made from brass, laten, iron and pewter. There was also still a glass industry, although it had reached its peak in the fifteenth century, when John Thornton was commissioned to create the great east window in York Minster.

Public entertainment was provided by strolling players and shows, and archery could be practised at the various butts – but 'roving' was favoured, shooting at targets scattered around the fields. The maypole, jack-in-the-green, street dancing, mummers' plays and wakes were the norm of yearly life. Felons found themselves in the city gaol which probably stood on the site of the later gaol, next to Trinity Church, and ended their days on the gallows (probably in Broadgate). Two such felons were the ambitious Pratt and South, who in 1523 planned to kill the mayor and council, rob St Mary's Hall and take Kenilworth Castle. Tried in London, these felons were sent to Coventry and hanged, drawn and quartered: their heads and limbs were displayed on New Gate, Bishop Gate, Bablake Gate and Greyfriars Gate. The city waits (instigated 1423) still wandered the night streets playing and singing melodious restful tunes, as they kept the night watch.

On Saturday 17 August 1565, Queen Elizabeth I came to Coventry during one of her state tours through the realm. The sheriffs, in scarlet coats, and twenty young men in purple livery, all on horseback, met the queen at the edge of the city county line, on the road to Wolvey. The group then rode before the queen's huge retinue of lords, ladies, soldiers, servants and baggage carts. As they approached the city they were met by the mayor, Edmund Brownell, and the aldermen of the city, all dressed in scarlet robes. The recorder, John Throckmorton, gave a welcoming speech and the mayor knelt by his side, holding the civic mace.

A nineteenth-century illustration showing Queen Elizabeth I riding through Broadgate on her visit to Coventry in August 1565

An engraving by Taunton showing Whitefriars. On her last day in Coventry tradition states that the queen addressed the people of Coventry from the oriel window

The recorder presented the queen with a Coventry-made red leather purse, containing £100 in gold angels. The queen on accepting the gift said:

'It is a good gift is £100 in gold, I have but few such gifts.' The mayor responded by saying:

'If you please your grace, there is a great deal more in it.'

'What is that?' asked the queen.

'The hearts of all your loving subjects' replied the mayor. Elizabeth replied, touched by this remark:

'We thank you, Mr Mayor, it is a great deal more indeed.'

The recorder remounted his horse and with the Earl of Huntingdon rode before the queen, leading the procession through Bishop Gate.

At the bottom of Bishop Street the queen dismounted and went into the grammar school, viewing the interior and its fine library. Then she presented money to the master for the upkeep of the institute. She then rode up to Broadgate and onwards to Whitefriars, where she stayed with John Hales.

On Sunday, Elizabeth watched a special performance of the mystery plays. The Tanners' pageant was at Spon Gate, the Drapers' in Cross

Cheaping, the Smiths' at Little Park Street, and the Weavers' at Much Park Street. A ring was also set up for bull-baiting, as the bull-ring outside the priory gate had fallen into disuse. Later the queen feasted with the Mayor and Corporation. The following day, before she left for Kenilworth, it is said the queen addressed the people of Coventry from the oriel window of Whitefriars. The royal retinue left via Spon Gate, accompanied by the Corporation to the County boundary, and on the following day attended her at Kenilworth, where the Recorder was knighted.

Another queen came to Coventry late in the evening on 25 November 1569. No celebrations marked her entry, for this was Mary, Queen of Scots. Suspected of being involved in murderous plots and losing out in various political manoeuvres, Mary, a Catholic, was driven from Scotland and became a thorn in Elizabeth's side as she claimed the throne as Elizabeth's rightful heir. Her presence in Protestant England worried Elizabeth, who reluctantly imprisoned the Scottish queen at Tutbury Castle. Catholic risings in the north forced Elizabeth to move Mary to the safety of Coventry. She wrote to the mayor and aldermen of the city:

> Trusty and wellbeloved we greet you well and forasmuch as we have for diverse good considerations given orders to our right trusty and right wellbeloved Cousins the Earls of Shrewsbury and Huntingdon to bring the Scottish Queen to that our town of Coventry, and there to see her safely kept and guarded until our pleasure shall be otherwise to determine, we let you with our pleasure and commandment is that for the better assistance of our said Cousins and either of them in this charge committed unto them, you shall from time to time follow such order and direction as shall for that purpose be by them presented unto you in such wise as they or either of them shall think fit for the weale and furtherance of our service. Given under our Signet at our Castle of Windsor the xxvi of November the xii year of our Reign.

Elizabeth ordered that Mary be confined in Coventry Castle but the earls, finding it ruinous, placed her in the Black Bull Inn in Smithford Street. The Earl of Shrewsbury promised to keep Mary out of sight, 'for the more she is seen the greater the danger'. The Earl of Huntingdon, knowing of the presence of Catholics in Warwickshire, felt uneasy and wrote to Lord Cecil, on 28 November: 'She lieth at an inn, where for me there is no lodging; her men also lie in the town, and go where they will.'

The 'Scotyshe Queene', Mary Queen of Scots, was brought to the city a prisoner and held in close confinement at St Mary's Hall

The queen responded angrily to the earls for 'carrying the Scottish Queen to an inn, which is very inconvenient'. She ordered that Mary be moved to a more secure place such as Greyfriars or a merchant's house, where the earls could also lodge, and to make sure she was never 'seen abroad on any pretence whatsoever'. Mary was then removed to St Mary's Hall and lodged within a room (later named Queen Mary's Room) in Caesar's Tower at the rear. Here she stayed under guard, served by her own people, and spent Christmas as a prisoner, returning to Tutbury in January 1570.

Elizabeth did not visit Coventry again, but the 'stout hearted men of Coventry' visited her during her celebrated visit to Kenilworth in 1575. On this royal visit the Earl of Leicester put on a show grander than any ever seen in England. Coventry men put on the city's noted Hock Tuesday play, a mock battle, which greatly amused the queen.

At this time, a young man called Michael Drayton (1563–1631) served as a page to Sir Henry Goodere, Member of Parliament for Coventry, who lived in a large house in Much Park Street. It was here that Drayton served the family and fell in love with Anne Goodere, eight years his junior. Sir Henry encouraged the young page in his talent for writing verse, and in later life Drayton found his way into the royal court, becoming friends with Shakespeare and Ben Jonson. Drayton's first fifty-one sonnets were published in 1594, under the title of *Idea's Mirror*, in honour of Anne. This was expanded in 1619 with a collection of poems, which included a 'Hymne to His Lady's Birthplace':

> Coventry, that do'st adorne
> The Countrey wherein I was borne

It continues in praise of Anne Goodere, referring to her birthday, 4 August 1571:

> Of thy streets which thou holdest best
> And most frequent of the rest, Happy Mich-Parke, every year
> On the fourth of August, there
> Let thy maids from Flora's bowers
> With their choice and daintiest flowers
> Deck them up, and from their store
> With brave garlands crown that door.

Drayton's love for Anne was either unrequited or never publicly acknowledged, for she married Sir Henry Rainford in 1596; but

Drayton and Anne remained friends for the rest of their lives. Drayton's work was prolific, with his greatest work being the *PolyOlbion*, a huge poetical work of 30,000 lines, describing countries, antiquities, flora and fauna. He was later rewarded with the position of poet laureate, and when he died, Drayton was buried in Poets' Corner in Westminster Abbey, under a long epitaph penned by Ben Jonson. The night before he died, Drayton wrote a poem for Anne beginning 'So well I love thee, as without thee I love nothing.' Drayton's connection with Shakespeare's death was recorded forty-six years after the event. It was said that after a heavy drinking session with Ben Jonson and Drayton, the Bard died from a fever.

Another gentleman of the quill, probably known to Shakespeare and Drayton, and certainly known by Jonson, who often argued with him, was John Marston, dramatist and satirist. Marston was born in Coventry in 1575, studied at Oxford and moved to London where his first work, *The Metamorphosis of Pygmalion's Image; and Certain Satires*, was published in 1598. A large number of dramas and comedies followed until he gave up writing in 1607, and shortly afterwards was ordained into the Church. Marston died in 1634.

A predecessor of Drayton and Marston is the slightly obscure figure of John Rastell, dramatist, who was born in Coventry and was Coroner from 1501 to 1508. Rastell married the daughter of Sir Thomas More, and was granted the estate of a burnt heretic after working for the diplomatic service in 1515. He specialized in plays and pageants, one of his better-known works being *The Four Elements*. Rastell died in prison in 1536, for opposing the right of the clergy to claim tithes.

In 1587 the city celebrated the execution at Fotheringay of its ex-prisoner, Mary, Queen of Scots. The population was counted, because of a shortage of provisions, and was found to be 6,502 – many thousands less than when the city was at the height of its prosperity before the Dissolution.

CHAPTER TWELVE

The Princess, the Plot and Prynne

Mary Queen of Scots was escorted to her death by Sir John Harington, owner of Coombe Abbey, and Recorder of Coventry. Six years later, on the death of the virgin queen, Sir John made preparation at his family seat at Exton for the coming of the newly proclaimed King James I from Scotland. His wife Elizabeth, through whom he had inherited Coombe, went to Edinburgh to acquaint herself with the new queen. The Haringtons won favour, and James's daughter, Princess Elizabeth, was invited to stay at Coombe while travelling to London. While there, Sir John brought the princess to Coventry, travelling in a coach. They were met on the Binley Road and brought to the city through Gosford Gate, then on to St Michael's where a sermon was preached. The princess was then taken across to St Mary's Hall where the party feasted, and the mayor presented her with a double-gilt silver cup, so tall and heavy that the little princess was unable to accept it without the help of Sir John.

In 1603 King James decided to let the Haringtons have the expensive honour of becoming guardians to the princess. The king promised to pay for her upkeep but kept pleading poverty, leaving Sir John deeply in debt. Coombe itself was turned into a fantasy land for the princess and other ladies of noble birth, who walked the grounds amid picturesque ruins and miniature horses and cattle. A visit to Coventry was, for a time, out of the question as plague raged through the city. It claimed 494 victims.

The year of 1605 saw Coombe and Coventry involved in an event of national importance, the Gunpowder Plot. The plot involved Catholic conspirators, led by Robert Catesby of Lapworth, who tried to blow up king and Parliament with the hope of placing Prince Henry or Princess Elizabeth on the throne, married to and controlled by Catholics. While Guy Fawkes was in London preparing for the destruction of the monarchy, Catholics began to gather in Warwickshire. Some stayed at the Black Bull Inn in Smithford Street

...mes I gave Sir John ...arington of nearby ...oombe Abbey the ...pensive honour of ...inging up his daughter. ...r presence had the city ...volved in a major ...ional incident – the ...npowder Plot

and others at the White Lion at Dunchurch. From these inns they met other Catholics on Dunsmore Heath under the guise of a hunting party, waiting to hear news of Fawkes's success.

The Gunpowder Plotters, many of whom were from Warwickshire Catholic families, met on Dunsmore Heath awaiting the news from London

The conspirators intended to ride on Coombe, and take the princess by force, but Sir John received a message that a known Catholic had stolen horses. Fearing rebellion, he quickly took the princess via back lanes to the safety of walled Coventry. She was lodged at the Hopkins's house in Earl Street, later known as the Palace Yard. Sir John and his retinue assisted by other Coventry men, rode to join the Sheriff of Warwickshire in pursuit of the conspirators, who scattered on hearing of Fawkes's capture. What followed became known as the Bloody Hunt of Dunsmore Heath, which ended with the capture and killing of many conspirators.

Elizabeth soon returned to the peace of Coombe, leaving when she married Frederick V. The wedding took place on St Valentine's Day, and was paid for by Sir John. As James owed Sir John so much, he offered him the right to strike farthings. Few were struck before Sir John died, massively in debt. It is interesting to note that when Elizabeth returned to England, after being exiled to Holland, she was looked after by William, Earl of Craven, who inherited Coombe from the Haringtons.

Prince Henry, the other intended victim of the Gunpowder Plot, visited Coventry in 1611. He was entertained at St Mary's Hall and presented with £50 in gold. His father, King James, followed on his way to Chester on 2 September 1617. The city prepared for his arrival by cleaning the streets and repainting the black and white timbered buildings. The king was met outside Bishop Gate by the mayor and aldermen dressed in scarlet. Dressed in black satin, Coventry's Philemon Holland, the 'Translator General' of many Greek and Latin works such as Pliny's *Natural History* and Camden's Britannia, made a long oration which was highly praised. The retinue then set off for St Mary's Hall, where a sumptuous feast had been laid. After this, James was presented with £100 inside a gold cup, weighing 45 ounces, of such fine Coventry craftsmanship that James promised to drink from it wherever he went. He ordered that his Coventry Cup be kept with the royal plate, so that it would be preserved for the heirs to the throne for ever. The king stayed the night at Whitefriars before heading for London.

On 18 July 1621 James I granted the city the Governing Charter, confirming all previous charters, and also granting two more fairs and setting up a closed corporation in the city. The new corporation consisted of a grand council of thirty-one members, appointed for life; from these men the mayor and aldermen were elected. The city was governed by this self-appointed council for 200 years. The Governing Charter was only issued when James had been assured that the people of Coventry, who had leanings towards Puritanism, received the sacrament on their knees as he had ordered in 1610.

The year of James's death, 1625, saw the last great visitation of the plague to Coventry. The numbers of dead do not seem to have been recorded, but many inhabitants moved from the city into temporary houses built in the Greyfriars Orchard and around Quinton Pool in Cheylesmore.

The crowning of Charles I that year had many repercussions in the city and the nation as a whole. His wife, Henrietta, was a practising Catholic in a land turning towards Puritanism, and Charles himself may also have been secretly practising the 'Old Faith'. Religion and politics went hand in hand in Stuart England, and king and parliament began to clash. Charles began to raise forced loans from towns and cities, Coventry included, without consulting Parliament. A number of citizens were imprisoned here for refusal of payment. With the introduction of a tax called ship money to help build up the royal fleet in 1635, Coventry's loyalty towards the monarch began to split, as the tax soon proved to be a source of personal revenue.

Discontent grew throughout the land. The king dissolved parliaments, as he believed in divine rule, and Archbishop Laud attacked

An engraving from the *Gentleman's Magazine* showing Coventry workmanship at its best: the Coventry Cup. James was so enthralled with it he promised to treasure it for the rest of his life

Puritanism. William Prynne, a puritan lawyer, wrote the *Histrio-matrix* (a scourge for actors), an attack on stage-plays, but some of it was considered an insult to the queen who liked to take part in masques herself. Prynne was found guilty of seditious writings and sentenced to be imprisoned, and to have his ears removed. Many were shocked at this act of barbarity and religious persecution, including the citizens of Coventry. When Prynne was being transported through Coventry, the mayor and citizens used the occasion to show their solidarity with the unfortunate lawyer. Prynne was welcomed as an honoured guest, and accompanied by the mayor to a service in his honour in St Michael's. For this act the mayor and corporation were later fined £200 by the privy council.

Meanwhile Charles I was creating turmoil in Scotland. Archbishop Laud forced a new prayer book on the Scots, and when it was read in Edinburgh riots broke out. Scotland defied the king's interference with the Deed of Covenant in defence of the 'true religion'. Charles's mis-handling of Scotland led to rebellion, then war. Soon the whole nation began to move towards civil war.

CHAPTER THIRTEEN

Civil War

B
y 22 August 1642, when Charles raised the royal standard at Nottingham, the English Civil War had officially begun.

Coventry began to build up its armoury as early as 1640. It was extended by private donations of arms; bills were repaired and new ones made, as were new pole-axes and pikes. 2 cwt of lead was cast into musket balls and over eight cwt was stored.

Two large bronze cannon called serpentines, two small iron cannon and a small piece of brass ordnance were 'new wheeled and stocked'. The serpentines and iron cannon were probably the pieces brought to Coventry from Bristol in 1450, during the Jack Cade rebellion scare.

In September 1640 fifty muskets and four barrels of gunpowder arrived from London, and the city was put on alert. The following year, in April, another fifty muskets, bandoliers and ten barrels of powder arrived. The armoury in St Mary's Hall now consisted of armour (mainly old), bows, bill-hooks, pikes, pole-axes, muskets, cannon, powder and balls. All the muskets were fixed to the wall and covered by a curtain some 10 1/2 yards long.

In January 1642 Christopher Davenport, the mayor, ordered that every householder should supply himself with arms, so that in time of threat at least 500 muskets could man the walls. An order of watch and ward was made, controlled by the aldermen of each ward; the watch lasted from 9 p.m. to 5 a.m. The council directed that no 'common or ordinarie' watchmen were to take on the task, only propertied able persons. The bar-gates were chained up every night and seventeen men guarded the gates; and all the minor gates and entrances were locked.

In March 1642 the Common Council ordered Alderman William Jesson MP to obtain four more cannon from Bristol, to add to the city's growing defences. War was near. Two months later the mayor received a letter from Sergeant Wightwick, Steward of Coventry Court, in Leicester, directing him and his sheriffs to attend the king at that city. The Council agreed to 'give satisfaction to his Majesty, that no prejudice shall happen against the city, or the liberties thereof.' Charles was obviously testing the loyalties of the central stronghold,

Charles I led England into civil war and tried to make Coventry his wartime capital

and the City Council feared the royal hand. The citizens of Coventry held no such fear, for on the Sunday morning as the mayor and sheriffs gathered to leave, a huge crowd stopped them.

Despite the anti-royalist feeling in the city, the Council still aimed to placate the king, for on 17 August, five days before the outbreak of war, a royal visit was expected. It was decided that £300 would be borrowed from Sergeant Wightwick and the mayor to entertain the king and the prince, and that 'a purse containing 200 pieces shall be presented to the king; and another purse with 100 pieces in it to the prince.'

On 18 August, as Charles rode through Warwickshire gathering forces, he received news from Coventry's recorder, Lord Northampton, that Parliamentary forces were going to occupy the city. Northampton informed Charles that he would make sure the city was held for him, and he secured the powder magazine in Spon Gate. Coventry's citizens showed their true colours, and Sergeant Wightwick and Aldermen Barker and Basnett gathered a force, retaking the magazine, which was moved to Warwick. Meanwhile, Northampton was trying to use his influence to turn the tide. He raised 400 men, but as he entered the Black Bull in Smithford Street, he was forced to flee for his life, leaving by the back entrance.

As King Charles approached the city via Stoneleigh, 400 men arrived from Birmingham to help Coventry in its defence of the Parliamentarian cause. Wishing to raise the royal standard here, and hearing that the city held rebels, Charles sent a message from Stoneleigh:

Whereas diverse persons ill affected to his Majesties person and government, and strangers to this City of Coventry, are lately gotten into that city with arms and ammunition, who, with others of that place ill affected to the peace of this Kingdom, have combined to keep the said City by force of arms against his Majesty, their Liege Lord and Sovereign. For reducing of whom to their due obedience his Majesty hath given orders to some Commanders of his Forces to assault the said City, and by force to enter the same. Notwithstanding his Majesty being very unwilling, for some disaffected persons, to punish his good subjects and ruin his said City, is graciously pleased thereby to declare, That in case the said Strangers shall forthwith, after the publishing of this His Proclamation, depart peaceably out of the said City and they and the inhabitants presently lay down their arms, that then his Majesty will pardon as well all the said strangers, as well as all other the Inhabitants of the said City. But if they shall persist in their said Action of Rebellion then his Majesty is resolved to proceed against them as Traitors and Rebels, and to use all extremity for reducing the said City to due obedience.

Given at our Court at Stonely Abbey the twentieth day of August, in the eighteenth year of our Reign, 1642.

On Saturday, 20 August 1642 the king and his army marched on Coventry. A herald in arms was sent ahead of the main force to demand entrance and was told by Dr Robert Phillips that 'his Majesty's royal person should be most respectfully welcomed, but we could not with safety permit his cavaliers to enter the town.' Knowing the king would not enter alone it was afterwards added that the king could enter with 200 of his followers. Charles, greatly angered at the snub, sent to Northampton for siege equipment and threatened to lay Coventry in ruins. He set up his cannons on the Park Hill and on the brow of Little Park Quarry. The main attack was against New Gate, by Whitefriars. Here concentrated fire caused a breach which the defenders blocked with carts and timber; despite continual attempts by the Royalists to break through, the defenders held the breach amid blasts of white billowing musket and cannon fire. King Charles watched the attack from The Mount, an artificial hill raised in 1627, near the present London Road cemetery. Stray cannon balls hit Whitefriars, and Lady Hales and an old lady who were in 'the Tower' were killed. One defender died during the attack, but this was said to have been due to his own carelessness. Some reports say that up to seventy Royalists were killed and taken prisoner.

Charles soon realized that Coventry was no easy target, and hearing that Lord Brooke's army was heading for Coventry, decided a strategic withdrawal was in order. His army headed for Nottingham, where the royal standard was raised. Three days later Lord Brooke arrived; those who had supported Northampton fled, or were sent as prisoners to Warwick.

Nicholas Wharton, a sergeant in one of the foot regiments led by Brooke, wrote to his late master in London. His first letter from Coventry is dated 26 August and says: 'Monday morning [22 August] we marched into Warwickshire with about three thousand foote and four hundred horse, until we came to Southam. This is a very malignant towne, both minister and people.' Wharton goes on to describe the occupation of the town. The vicarage was ransacked and weapons confiscated, and when the troops were quartering themselves an alarm

was given, with cries of 'Arm, arm, the enemy is coming.' All came to arms but no enemy arrived. In the early hours of the morning, however, 800 cavalry and 300 foot appeared led by Lord Northampton, Lord Carnarvon, Lord Compton and Captain Legge. The Parliamentarians, with 'a few troops of horse and six field pieces', opened fire upon the Royalists, killing many of them. The Royalists fled, taking most of their dead, but 'Several dead corps were in corne fields, amongst them a trumpeter, whose trumpet our horsemen sounded into Coventry.'

Wharton's next letter, dated 30 August, tells us more:

My last was unto you from Coventry, August the 26th, which place is still one quarter; a City invironed with a wall co-equal, if not exceedinge that of London for breadth and height; the compass of it is near three miles, all of free stone. It hath four strong gates, stronge battlements, stored with towers, bulwarks, and other neces-saries. This city hath magnificent churches and stately streets; with-in it ther are also several and pleasant sweete springes of water built of free stone, very large, sufficient to supply many thousand men. The City gates are guarded day and night with four hundred armed

The defenders of Coventry held back against the Royalist onslaught, holding the breach in the wall at Newgate. The Sealed Knot in action

men, and no man entreth in or out but upon open examination. It is also very sweetly situate. Thursday, August 26th, our soldiers pillaged a malignant fellowes house in this City and the Lord Brooke immediately proclaimed that whosoever should for the future offend in that kind should have martiall law. Fryday several of our soldiers both horse and foote sallyed out of the City unto Lord Dunsmore's parke [Kings Newnham] and brought from thence great store of venison, which is good as ever I tasted and ever since they make it their dayley practise, so that venison is almost as common with us as beef with you. This day our horsemen sallyed out, as their daily custom is, and brought in with them two cavaleers and with them an old base Priest [George Dale] the parson of [Walsgrave-on] Sowe, near us, and led him rediculously about the city unto the chief Commanders. Sunday morne the Lord Essex, his chaplain Mr Kemme, the cooper's sonne, preached unto us, and this was the first sermon we heard since we came from Ailsbury; but before he had ended his first prayer Newes was brought into the Church [St Michael's] unto our commanders that Nuneaton some six miles from us, was fired by the enemy, and forthwith our Generall and severall captaines issued forth but I and many others stayed until sermon was ended, after which we were commanded to march forth with all speed, namely my captain with Captain Beacon and Captain Francis of our regiment, and of other regiments, in all to the number of one thousand foote, and one troope of horse, but before we came at them they all ran away, not having done much harm whereupon we returned to Coventry again.

The Cavaliers who fled were led by the king's nephew, Prince Rupert of the Rhine, who had tried to place Caldecote Hall under siege. Thirty prisoners were taken after Rupert's men fled the field thinking they were under cannon fire; the blasts and billowing smoke were caused, in fact, by several muskets tied to a gun carriage.

Wharton's next letter was dated 3 September, and was written before his regiment left the city: 'Wensday [31 August] wee kept the fast and heard two sermons, but before the third was ended we had an alarm to march presently. By ten of the clock we got our regiments together and kept our rendevow in the City until midnight, and about two in the morning marched out of this City towards Northampton. This City hath four steeples, three churches, two parishes, and not long since but one priest: but now the world is well amended with them.'

Nicholas Wharton and his regiment marched on 19 September, stopping at Baginton, then moved to Warwick; later they marched to battle at Edgehill in October 1642. When the king had retreated from Coventry to Nottingham, he had left two companies of foot and one of horse at 'Killingworth' (Kenilworth) Castle. Later, as the 'power of the rebels in that countie did dalie increase,' the king sent troops to bring the companies back to safety. This rescue party was led by Sir William Dugdale who knew the country lanes well. The Royalists left Kenilworth in the early morning with wagons of ammunition, gun-powder and stores. News quickly reached Coventry, and troopers flooded out to intercept the 'malignants'. The encounter took place on Curdworth Heath, near Coleshill and, although outnumbered, the Parliamentarian troops put the Royalists to flight, taking a number of prisoners.

Robert Devereux, Earl of Essex, Coventry's Recorder and successful general in the Parliamentarian forces

Coventry was now under military rule, with a large permanent garri-son. The Earl of Northampton was thrown out of office, and Robert Devereux, Earl of Essex and general of the Parliamentary army, was made Coventry's new recorder. Trading was suspended and shops closed, for all was controlled by the governor of the garrison. Noting an increase in Royalist activity, Essex ordered more troops and cannon to Coventry, to hold it in case of siege. The city now held over 4,000 troops, had its own citizens' militia and more cannon.

It is said that on 14 October 1642 Prince Rupert arrived with his cavalry and with his usual manic bravado attacked. His force was quickly repulsed, but not before a number of Cavaliers had entered the city. The horsemen were quickly dispatched as they found themselves trapped by carts in narrow streets. Rupert retreated back to the coun-tryside, and nine days after fought with the king against Essex and Cromwell at the battle of Edgehill.

A seventeenth-century woodcut of the king's nephew, Prince Rupert of the Rhine. He, like his uncle, led an unsuccessful attack on the city

As the Parliamentarian army headed south, prisoners were lodged in Coventry and eighteen wagon-loads of provisions were sent to them. As provisions would be needed to prepare for possible siege, the inhabitants were counted: 9,500 people. Grain was stored, and an extra defensive tower was added between New Gate and Little Park Gate. This new five-sided tower, built to defend a blind spot, contained a number of port-holes through which a number of cannon gave a lethal coverage of fire-power.

1643 began with the election of Alderman Barker as Governor of Coventry and Colonel of its militia and cavalry. The old moat was dug out again around the city wall, and new sluices joined it to the rivers Sherbourne and Albert. All buildings and trees within gunshot of the city wall were removed. These included buildings in Bishop Street, Gosford Street, Spon Street, Hill Street, and outside New Gate. To make up for this loss, buildings were erected at New Buildings (giving it its name), Greyfriars Lane and St Agnes Lane. All the gates were blocked up, except for New Gate, Gosford Gate and Spon Gate. Outside these gates defensive ditches were dug, with outer half-moon ramparts; each gate was given a drawbridge, and one or more cannon, ready charged for instant use.

Barrs Hill was fortified to help protect the north side, but this fortification soon proved awkward to maintain. The women of Coventry filled in the quarries in the Great Park, so they could not afford shelter to the enemy, and at night 120 men watched from the city wall. To accommodate the increase in prisoners, the Leather Hall in West Orchard was adapted to hold ordinary prisoners, while the more important captives were held in the Head Marshal's House, near Whitefriars Gate in Much Park Street. Coventry was a bustling place; in fact it began to get overcrowded as it attracted more and more into the safety of its walls. This caused problems, and many strangers were expelled. Troops regularly rode out to oversee the countryside, and Royalists avoided the area, knowing Coventry's power.

Governor Alderman Barker was elected mayor in 1644. It is said that under his mayoral robes he always wore his buff leather coat and sword, and on civic occasions he was attended by his officers. Even when proclaiming the city fair he was accompanied by a troop of cavalry.

The following year saw the Royalist army take Leicester for the king. This put Coventry on full alert, and work began on an outwork outside Gosford Gate, encompassed by the river. Coventry's Recorder, the Earl of Essex, was not ruthless enough, despite his many successes as a general, and was forced to resign his leadership. Parliament began to create the New Model Army based on Cromwell's 'Ironsides'. This force, led by Sir Thomas Fairfax and Cromwell, met the royal army at Naseby on 14 July, utterly defeating the Royalists and practically ending the Civil War. Charles, meanwhile, fled to Wales.

In 1646 the Scottish 11th Regiment of Foot, under Parliament, came to Coventry and encamped on King's Field by Gosford Green, where provisions were sent out to them. In January 1647 Parliament paid part of the regiment's wages and it headed home. Charles, who had earlier tried to negotiate with the Scots, was left in the hands of Parliament.

The Earl of Essex died on 14 September 1647, and on 1 November Basil Fielding, the Earl of Denbigh and Major-General of Coventry, was sworn in as the city's new recorder. Denbigh continued in office for four years. It is interesting to note that at the battle of Edgehill he fought against his own father, who led Royalist troops. This divided family loyalty was echoed throughout the land.

In April 1648 the Second Civil War broke out, with Royalist uprisings in Kent and Wales. These were quickly put down by Cromwell and Fairfax. In August a Scottish army of Royalists headed south, but at Preston they were attacked by Cromwell. Half of the army fled to Scotland, while the other half was forced to surrender. Large numbers of prisoners were taken, several hundred of whom were brought to Coventry and imprisoned in Bablake church (St John's), the Leather Hall, Spon Gate and Greyfriars Gate.

It was due to the confinement of such prisoners that the phrase 'Sent to Coventry' is thought to have originated; when Coventrians refused to talk to the prisoners, they were snubbed, 'sent to Coventry'. This may not be the original meaning of the expression, for as we have seen in previous chapters being 'sent to Coventry' could often be a one way trip. It is interesting that Covintree means the tree of punishment, a tree of mass hangings. Covent Garden in London was a royal execution ground, as was Coventry. The earliest recorded execution in Coventry was during the reign of Henry III (1216–72). When staying at Woodstock, King Henry discovered a priest named Riband attempting to enter his chamber by night. The priest admitted he had been hired to kill the king, and was sentenced to be 'sent to Coventry' and there 'torne by wild horses, and drawn thro' the streets till life leave bodie'. This being done, his remains were scattered around the land as a warning to would-be regicides.

In January 1649 Charles, finally defeated by Cromwell, was taken to Westminster Hall and put on trial. One of those who found the king guilty of tyranny was Colonel William Purefoy of Caldecote Hall, Warwickshire. Purefoy became Recorder of Coventry in October 1651, and ordered that his wage for the position should be used to repair the windows of Bablake church (then a meeting place for the Independents) which had been defaced by the Scottish prisoners held there after the battle of Preston. Colonel Purefoy is said to have died in 1659, but he probably simply disappeared – for as one of the regicides he must have felt threatened by the restoration of Charles II.

Coventry had now ceased to be a fully garrisoned city and war had ended. A new England was about to be born.

CHAPTER FOURTEEN

Commonwealth and Restoration

T he execution of Charles I left Parliament and the army in total control. England became a republic. On 23 December 1653 Oliver Cromwell was declared Lord Protector of England, and in Coventry this was celebrated with church bells, trumpets, drums and bonfires.

When Cromwell died in 1658 his son Richard, a kindly man, did not have the power of character or the inclination to rule. Two Parliamentary generals, Lambert and Fleetwood, began to clamour for power and forced Richard to abdicate. They then set up the Committee of Safety, thus controlling the army and attempting to rule England. In 1659 twenty-three members of the Committee of Safety arrived in Coventry to take control, and the mayor feared that the city would be turned into a 'seat of warr'. Mayor Hicks ordered the magazine in St Mary's Hall to be broken open, and a group of armed men gathered in St Michael's churchyard. They then marched on the main guard at the Cross and demanded, and were given, the guard of the city. Coventry was declared for a free Parliament against Lambert and Fleetwood.

Lambert began to march north, but as the threat of battle with the armies of General Monk in Scotland and Fairfax in Yorkshire drew near his men deserted him, and he was taken prisoner. On taking control of London, Monk decided to fulfil the people's wishes, and declare for a free Parliament, opening the way for the Restoration.

The restoration of Charles II was declared in Coventry on 10 May 1660 by the mayor, Thomas Basnet, from the Cross in Cross Cheaping. Drums and trumpets sounded, as several companies of infantry, and two of horse, fired volleys from the base of the Cross.

To win favour the Corporation sent a deputation to London, to present Charles with a silver basin and ewer, fifty pieces of gold and rents formerly paid to the Crown. On 8 October James, Earl of Northampton, Coventry's former recorder, was returned to office. He and a number of local gentry arrived in the city on 31 October, and on the following day Northampton was sworn in, and feasted at the mayor's house.

Charles was crowned on St George's Day 1661, and Coventry celebrated with bells, bonfires and feasts, and claret ran from the conduits.
The king's restoration also meant the restoration of the Church of
England. As Lichfield had been Royalist during the war it was rewarded: the restored bishopric was named Lichfield and Coventry, rather
than Coventry and Lichfield, and Coventry was ordered to pay
towards the restoration of war-damaged Lichfield cathedral.

In 1678 Lady Godiva made her first appearance in the procession
which heralded the Show Fair. This ancient procession, led by St
George, men in armour and the mayor and council grew more flam-
boyant, and later became known as the Godiva Procession.

In September 1682 the king's illegitimate son, James, Duke of
Monmouth, stayed at the Palace Yard. Monmouth was a popular rival
to the Duke of York (later James II) in his claim to the throne. On the
night of his arrival bells rang and bonfires lit his way to the inn. The
mayor refused to have anything to do with Monmouth, who spent the
night feasting at the Palace Yard, among ex-Parliamentarians.
Monmouth visited the mayor's parlour the following morning, amid a
crowd shouting, 'A Monmouth – No York!' Here he drank a glass of
wine and spoke with the mayor before leaving, surrounded by cheer-
ing people. Three years after this visit Monmouth was banished for
plotting against the throne, and in 1686 he was beheaded after leading
a rebellion in the south.

James II visited Coventry on 1 September 1687. He was met by
over 200 horsemen and brought into the city via Spon Gate. On enter-
ing he was presented with the customary gold cup. The king then sur-
prised all by handing the gift to Lord Dartmouth saying, 'I would have
your Lordship receive this cup and cover as a mark of the City of
Coventry's concern for your father.' Dartmouth's father, Colonel
Legge, was held prisoner in the city after the battle of Worcester, until
he escaped dressed in his wife's clothes. This royal rebuke brought an
end to Coventry's customary gift of the golden cup.

James stayed at the Palace Yard despite being expected at
Whitefriars. That night he feasted with supporters of his Act of
Indulgence, which gave freedom of religious worship. Little did they
know that the act was passed to ensure the return of the Catholic faith.
This would later cause a bloodless revolution, forcing James to flee.

The following day James visited Coventry Cross and the city's
churches, ending at St Michael's where he touched 300 people to cure
the 'King's Evil'. Afterwards he feasted at St Mary's Hall, where his
table was so full of food that it collapsed under the weight. James left
the city via New Gate, escorted by the mayor and company. Among

The Duke of Monmouth
stayed at the Palace Yard
in Earl Street (almost
directly opposite St
Mary's Lane). After his
execution it was realized
that no painting of him
existed, and it is reputed
that his head was stitched
back on so that an artist
could do the honours. This
illustration is based on
that painting

James II snubbed
Coventry's customary gift
of the golden cup, thus
ending a long tradition

The Palace Yard in Earl Street. Like previous royalty Princess Anne stayed at this mansion. One of Coventry's finest fifteenth-century houses it was destroyed on the night of the Coventry blitz, 14 November 1940

the royal retinue was William Penn, the founder of Pennsylvania.

The unpopular rule of James came to an end when William of Orange was invited to deliver the country from Catholic rule. After William's landing, Princess Anne (later queen) escaped from confinement and joined his supporters at Nottingham. She came to Coventry on 11 December 1688; and she, her noblemen and 1,000 horsemen were met at Bishop Gate by the mayor, council and populace. Anne spent two days in the city before leaving for Warwick.

In 1690 thousands of English, Dutch, German and French troops and cavalry passed through and stayed in the city, on their way to Ireland, where James was trying to raise support. William himself passed through on 3 June, on the way to join his army. After his victory at the battle of the Boyne great celebrations ensued in Coventry.

CHAPTER FIFTEEN

From Silk to Soldiers

The simple hand-loom could be found in weavers' homes and in small factories. It is to this machine and the sweat of the weaver that Coventry owed much of its prosperity

A t the end of the seventeenth century Coventry was a prosperous and growing city, with a population numbering nearly 9,000. Despite this, eighteenth-century Coventry had no royal visits and had no bearing on national events. More a market town than a city, it began to grow with the large-scale introduction of silk ribbon weaving, by Mayor William Bird. Bird set up a ribbon weaving works in 1705, probably with the help of French Huguenots. By 1756 he employed 2,000 hand-loom weavers. Other manufacturers sprang up, and soon Coventry found itself the ribbon capital of the Midlands. Ribbons were chiefly black in the early part of the century, but by the end of the century a rainbow of colours poured forth.

By the middle of the century clock and watchmaking was firmly established. Samuel Vale started watchmaking in 1747, and later went

An engraving by Taunton of eighteenth-century Broadgate looking north. Most of these fine buildings were destroyed when Broadgate was widened in 1820

Drawing based on a 1799 illustration by Rowlandson. The view shows the King's Head near the top of Smithford Street. One of the city's premier coaching inns, it was also the favourite billet of army officers before the barracks was built

into partnership with Richard Rotherham. Vale and Rotherham became the city's largest and most famed watchmaker and lasted for about 200 years.

Since the Civil War, parliamentary elections had become increasingly complex and advanced considerably. Whereas before candidates who represented the city had its common good in mind, each party was now politically motivated. This resulted in the misuse of power, and disorderly elections, for which Coventry became notorious. In 1722 an election riot took place when the Tories blocked the entrance to the polling-booth. The Whigs gathered, and the resulting brawl cleared the way for the voting freemen. The election of 1780 reached the zenith of electoral disputes. The mayor secretly swore in sixty-six new freemen on the understanding that they would vote for the Whig candidate. 'Several hundred colliers, roughs and prize-fighters' were brought in to keep the peace for the Whigs, and they immediately took possession of the polling booth in Cross Cheaping. In support of the Tory candidate, Lord Craven hired hundreds of 'ruffians and clodhoppers', who marched from Coombe armed with clubs and bludgeons. The resulting pitched battle called the Bludgeon Fight ended with a large number of colliers barricaded in St Mary's Hall, as stones were thrown through the ancient windows.

The Women's Market in the early nineteenth century, unchanged since Wesley's time. The site later became the Market Hall and Market Square; it was destroyed in the blitz and is now the site of the Hotel Leofric

This dispute was reported in Coventry's first newspaper. Called *Jopson's Coventry Mercury*, the four-page newspaper, printed by J. Jopson in Hay Lane, first appeared on Monday, 20 July 1741. It appeared until 1836, when it became the *Coventry Standard*.

On Tuesday, 12 August 1755 the Park became the venue for Coventry Races. Here, before thousands of spectators, horses ran for cups and cash prizes. The first race for a purse of £50 went to a grey called 'Maggot'. The following year Lord Byron's grey hunter, 'Lightning', came third in a race. After the races, balls were held. These made Coventry Races an important event on Warwickshire's social calendar. The races ended in 1783, when a horse and rider lost control, jumped a stile by Little Park Gate and killed a seven-year-old girl.

Also in 1755, one of Coventry's most extraordinary mayors came to office for the first of three times. Alderman John Hewitt, junior, a silkman, began his mayoralty with a magnificent feast at St Mary's Hall. Hewitt was a leading thief-taker, having a spy system throughout the county, and often pursuing criminals down to London itself. His long memory and relentlessness made him into one of the finest thief-takers in Georgian England. Throughout his career Hewitt was responsible for the apprehension, and sometimes execution, of hundreds of criminals, murderers and highwaymen.

In his journals Hewitt noted the arrival in 1756 of 600 soldiers whom he was responsible for billeting. This included ten officers, who were billeted at the King's Head. These men belonged to General

Stewart's 37th Regiment of Foot. During their long stay in the city, forty-seven pressed men joined them and a number of other men deserted. One such was shot against the wall by Little Park Gate in April 1757. On 23 June another deserter received 1,000 lashes and was drummed out of the regiment with a halter around his neck. Two days later Private George Robinson was shot for the same offence and for selling parts of his kit to entertain ladies of easy virtue.

The newly formed Coventry Canal Company held its first meeting in 1768 at the White Bear Inn (later the Craven Arms) in the High Street, one of Coventry's coaching inns, which had been running regular coaches to London since 1750. A year later the first boats of coal arrived from Bedworth on the newly opened canal. This would be the main transportation system for goods until the coming of the railway.

In 1779 the father of Methodism, John Wesley, visited Coventry. The mayor refused Wesley permission to preach in St Mary's Hall, giving preference to a dancing master. His followers had a small room in a building by the Women's Market, but Wesley preached from under the cover on the Market House as he drew such large crowds. Wesley was so successful that he returned in 1782 and 1786.

France declared war on England in 1793, and Napoleon threatened invasion. England began to set up barracks in key towns, and in Coventry the Government purchased the medieval Black Bull Inn and its extensive grounds for £2,025, so that it could be converted into barracks. There were two entrances, following the original entrances to the Bull – one a stone archway bearing the royal arms in Smithford Street, and the other at the bottom of Hertford Street at what is now Bull Yard.

The medieval Black Bull Inn probably dated from the fourteenth century. In modern times it stood just over halfway down the Upper Precinct. The huge grounds of the Bull became the Coventry Barracks, then the Barracks Market and are now the Barracks car park

Through most of its life Coventry Barracks was the home to cavalry regiments. This photograph taken in the late 1860s shows lancers standing by captured cannon from the Crimea. These cannon were later used as features on Greyfriars Green and Swanswell Park

By the entrance were the officers' quarters, and on either side were offices leading to the main parade ground, which had stabling either side, above which were housed the soldiers. Around the square were various buildings including stores, hospital and guard-house.

The first occupants of these cavalry barracks were the newly formed Coventry Volunteers. From the late 1790s came troops of cavalry, dragoons, hussars and lancers, with their splendid uniforms. These mounted troops became part of daily life, regularly exercising on Greyfriars Green or in the Park, practising with sword and lance at full gallop, watched by crowds of admiring girls and children. In the late 1860s the Royal Field Artillery arrived followed by the 7th Battalion of the Royal Warwickshire Regiment, who were stationed here before leaving for France in the First World War, when it effectively fell from use. In 1922 the barracks became a market, and now the site is occupied primarily by the Barracks car park.

Over the last hundred years the population had risen to about 15,000. This increase was mainly due to the silk and watch industries, and the permanent military force. Coventry was now a garrison town and would remain so for the next hundred years.

CHAPTER SIXTEEN

Industrial Decline and Rebirth

T he nineteenth century arrived with a nationwide shortage of wheat and other foodstuffs, which led to rapid inflation in the cost of living. Anger at these events caused many Coventrians to riot, but this was soon put down by the use of the military, and the recently formed Coventry Volunteers. Hardship continued for some years, and the number of poor in the city increased. Whitefriars was turned into a workhouse to accommodate them, and in 1809 thousands of gallons of soup, 23,520 loaves and 23,088 lbs of meat were distributed.

During this period the city had three notable visitors. The first, on 3 September 1802, was Lord Nelson, accompanied by Lady Hamilton and her husband. This surprise visit caught the Council unaware and they rushed to meet his carriage as it arrived at the King's Head. The next visitor was the Prince of Wales (later George IV) in 1807, on his way to visit Earl Craven at Coombe Abbey. When passing up the narrow Greyfriars Lane, then the main entrance from the south-west, his carriage was delayed because of the traffic. The Prince commented that he hoped this would be remedied before his next visit, and when he visited Earl Craven again, in 1817, his carriage passed along Hertford Street, which had been built in 1812–13. The third visitor was the exiled Louis XVIII of France, who stayed at the King's Head in 1808. He was finally placed back on the throne of France by the Duke of Wellington, who himself stayed at the King's Head in 1823.

Coventry's silk-weaving industry continued to grow, as did the population, which by 1821 had reached 21,242. The city had not expanded in size, but there was new building in the grounds of larger houses. This produced the once common Coventry courts. The city attracted more and more 'foreigners' (mainly Warwickshire people) to its growing industries, but often the citizens outnumbered the jobs. Unrest began to grow as new machinery began to displace some workers. Weavers formed groups to fight for higher wages and often found themselves imprisoned.

A large number of Coventry weavers were out-workers; their looms were worked in the once common Coventry 'top shop'. The introduction of the steam loom threatened the survival of the outworker

A notorious incident took place on 7 November 1831, when weavers gathered to discuss wage levels. One such group, numbering about seven hundred, gathered at the Mill Dam Pool at the bottom of New Buildings to complain about Josiah Beck, who had introduced the first steam looms into his small factory (a three-storied house with workshops above) in New Buildings. His workshop had already suffered attacks from weavers who saw that the steam loom threatened their livelihoods.

Soon a 500-strong mob marched up the hill to Beck's workshop. The ringleaders hammered on Beck's yard door until he answered, and asked to see the looms. As Beck allowed them in, the mob rushed forward, attacking him with stones and forcing him to climb the neighbouring wall. The mob began to smash the looms and steam engine, and set fire to the premises. Beck was abused by the mob until he finally escaped and the military broke up the riot. Among the few arrests were Benjamin Sparks aged twenty, Thomas Burbury, twenty-nine, and Alfred Toogood, seventeen, who were all sentenced to death. They were later reprieved, however, and transported to Australia for life. It is ironic that Josiah Beck died, a poor inmate at Bablake almshouse, aged eighty-four, in 1876, while Alfred Toogood became a respectable, rich Australian gentleman.

By 1834 trade unionism was well established in the city. In March the funeral of a union leader took place at Foleshill, and his coffin was followed by 1,500 union members and several thousand spectators.

Crowds of thousands also gathered for Coventry Races, which restarted at Stoke in 1830, and in 1852 moved to Crampers Field in

The Godiva Procession followed by the Great Fair had since the late seventeenth century been a major event in the Coventry calendar. The Godiva ride brought thousands of curious spectators into the city and was a very profitable event. This view shows the junction of Broadgate, Smithford and Hertford Streets

Radford. The course was considered one of the best mile courses in the country, and was well attended. Races were discontinued for a short time, then revived in October 1874 when the famed Fred Archer rode Anina to victory in the Packington Nursery Plate.

Another great crowd puller was the prize-fight. Coventry's most noted pugilist was William 'Paddy' Gill, who fought his first fight, for £5, on Radford Common in 1838. Paddy took on and beat all local opposition, and soon began to take on national fighters. His penultimate fight for £200 near Bagshott in 1850 ended after fifty-three rounds with a knock-out, from which his opponent, Thomas Griffiths, died. Paddy ended his days as landlord of the Lamp Tavern in Market Street. Other city prize-fighters were John 'Fatty' Adrian, who kept the Windmill in Spon Street and later the Pitts Head in Gosford Street; Bob Randle, who kept the Woolpack in St John's Street; and 'Gameun' Shilton, 'Ginger' Berry and Bill Heap, all weavers and butchers.

The Municipal Corporations Act of 1835 led to the end of the closed council which had been in existence since 1621. The council was now open to any freeman or property owner and new elections were called. During these parliamentary elections, known as the Bloody Tenth, hundreds of Tory and Whig supporters fought running battles in the streets. The Tories were driven into the King's Head, their election headquarters, the yard of which was described as having the 'appearance of a slaughterhouse'. This was the last of the old notorious city elections and soon politics superseded violence.

In 1838 Coventry was connected to London and Birmingham by rail after many years of work. The track followed a line specified by George Stephenson, said to have walked the route three times.

Coventry's most notable resident in the nineteenth century was Mary Ann Evans, better known by her pen-name, George Eliot. She received the latter part of her education (1832–5) at a private school in Warwick Row. When her mother was ill in 1835, Mary Ann returned home to Griff House, Arbury, to nurse her, and when her mother died in the following year, kept house for her father, who paid a teacher to tutor her.

In March 1841 Robert Evans left Griff House to his son, and with Mary Ann moved to Bird Grove, a large semi-detached house off the rural Foleshill Road. Their neighbours, Abijah and Elizabeth Pears, soon introduced Mary Ann to Charles and Caroline Bray, who lived at Rosehill (site of the Coachmakers' Club) in Radford. Bray, a ribbon manufacturer, philosopher, reformer, writer and free-thinker had turned his home into a meeting place for 'thinkers' of the time. There were many famous visitors, including Dickens, Thackeray, Cobden and Bright.

Mary Ann Evans, better known as novelist George Eliot. Coventry was a very important factor in this great writer's life. In fact it could be said that George Eliot, the writer, was born in Coventry

Mary Ann began to visit the Brays regularly, and soon told her father that she could not attend church, as she no longer believed. Her shocked father sent her back to Griff, away from the influence of the Brays. Both were unhappy, and friends convinced Robert to let Mary Ann come back, on the understanding that she attended church with him.

The Rosehill set introduced Mary Ann to the literary world, and her first step towards literary fame was a translation of 'Das Leben Jesu'. In 1846 Charles Bray bought the *Coventry Herald* as a political mouthpiece, and encouraged Mary Ann to write essays and reviews in it. Robert Evans died in 1849 and the Brays took Mary Ann to the continent, leaving her at Geneva until the spring, when she returned to Rosehill. Shortly after her return she was invited to write an article for the *Westminster Review*. After a few more visits to Rosehill, Mary Ann moved permanently to London where her literary career grew from strength to strength. Despite leaving Coventry for good she never lost touch with the Brays, writing to them for the rest of her life. Her novels often reflected her past: the setting of *Middlemarch* is based on Coventry, and St Mary's Hall appears in *Adam Bede*. Charles Bray appears as Charles Raymond and Coventry as Coventford. It is interesting to note that a retired ribbon manufacturer lived in Foleshill at this time; his name was George Elliot.

Bird Grove, the then semi-rural home of Robert and Mary Ann Evans. Their neighbours in this splendid semi-detached house, the Pears, introduced Mary Ann to the Brays

New ratings which became applicable after the Municipal Act caused disputes with the villages that formed the County of Coventry. This was resolved with the Coventry Boundary Act of 1842 which abolished the County of the City of Coventry, taking Coventry back into Warwickshire. The gaol and County Hall thereafter were transferred to the control of the Justices of the Peace for Warwickshire.

On 15 December 1856 Charles Dickens visited Coventry, and read his *A Christmas Carol* for charity before an enthralled audience in the newly opened Corn Exchange in Hertford Street (later the Empire cinema, demolished in the 1960s). He returned on 5 December 1858, as guest of honour at a dinner held at the Castle Hotel in Broadgate, and was presented with a specially engraved Coventry watch, which he used for the rest of his life. While here, Dickens visited the Rotherham watch factory in Spon Street, St Michael's church and St Mary's Hall. In this same year Queen Victoria was received by the mayor and council at Coventry Station. After the official greeting the queen left for Stoneleigh.

Nineteenth-century copperplate etching showing Coventry as a city which had hardly grown from within the boundary laid down by its now long gone city wall. Early industry is represented by the appearance of factory chimneys

* * *

The import duty on French and Swiss ribbons was abolished in 1860, and large quantities were imported. Around the same time America placed a heavy import duty on ribbons. The trade in Coventry began to

suffer as a result of these factors, and especially because the ribbon was going out of fashion. Coventry's ribbon factories stopped giving outwork to home weavers and workers were made redundant: thousands of weavers were applying for charity. Those weavers who were still working were offered lower wages and went on strike. This lasted until most faced starvation. They tried to return to work, only to find that the industry had collapsed and no work was available. Thousands found themselves unemployed; the city's population at the time (1861) was 41,638: of these 25,000 were skilled in the weaving trade and 2,037 in watchmaking. Many lived off hand-outs and the soup kitchen in St Mary's Hall; others emigrated to America, Canada, Australia and New Zealand. In 1861 alone, 4,000 left the city to emigrate.

Although the factories survived this loss, the 'outworkers' of the City Centre, Hillfields and many rural areas did not fare so well. Lord Leigh set up Leigh Mills in Hill Street to help, and by 1900 there were around 2,000 weavers left, many of whom worked for J. and J. Cash, whose cottage factories still survive at Kingfield, Radford.

In the hot summer of 1861, as unemployed weavers stood on street corners watching the world go by, a gentleman arrived who would revive the ailing city. That man was James Starley, who together with Josiah Turner, and others from London, launched the Coventry Sewing Machine Company, making Starley's improved machines. The venture was successful and Starley's machines began to be exported world-wide. In 1866 Turner sent his nephew over to France as his

England's greatest novelist, Charles Dickens, used Coventry as a basis for part of his novel *The Old Curiosity Shop*. An unusually tall timbered building in Little Butcher Row was in the nineteenth century called Ye Olde Curiositie Shoppe

Leigh Mills in Hill Street (now site of Leigh Mills car park) was built at the personal expense of Lord Leigh of Stoneleigh Abbey to help the city's collapsed economy. The mill supplied work for Coventrians well into the twentieth century

ames Starley, father of
he cycle industry. A
ussex farm boy whose
nventive genius helped
ut Coventry back on to
he road to prosperity

Coventry watches formed
one of the staple trades of
he city but suffered from
cheap inferior imports.
These watches which
vere famous for their
accuracy are now
xtremely rare

agent, to investigate the 'boneshakers' that were popular there, and was asked to bring one back from Paris. In 1868 Turner's nephew caused quite a stir as he rode the machine from Coventry Station to the factory in King Street.

With the production of cycles in mind, the firm's name was changed to the Coventry Machinist Co. Ltd, and soon Starley began to work on improving the bicycle. He worked on various ideas and discussed the problems with William Hillman (later of Hillman cars), and in 1870 took out a patent with Hillman on a penny farthing called the Ariel, the first all-metal cycle. Starley patented improvement after improvement, and after falling off his four-wheeled Wonder into stinging nettles when cycling up Knightlow Hill in Stretton on Dunsmore, he pulled out pencil and paper and invented the differential gear, now found in all vehicles.

In June 1881 Starley was commanded to attend the queen at Windsor with two of his Salvo Quad tricycles. He was presented with an engraved watch and permission to rename the trike the 'Royal Salvo'. These were the first machines to use chains, and rack and pinion steering.

Later in the summer of 1881 James Starley died, aged fifty-one, at home in Upper Well Street, of cancer of the liver. Shortly before he died, his wife discovered him smashing up a highly advanced prototype sewing machine. Knowing he would not live to complete and patent the machine, Starley destroyed it in a fit of desperate frustration.

Starley was considered by many to have been the saviour of Coventry, for he brought new industries and prosperity to the city. To honour the 'Father of the Cycle Industry', a monument was unveiled in Queens Grove before 8,000 people. All modern cycles are based on the Rover, invented by Starley's nephew John Kemp Starley.

By the 1890s over 40,000 people worked in the cycle trade. Apart from the major firms, such as Rudge, Singer, Humber, Hillman, Starley Bros, Swift and Triumph, Coventry was home to 248 cycle manufacturers between the 1860s and 1930s, making the city the largest cycle manufacturer in the world. As this trade grew, the city's watch trade, which had been in existence for 300 years, began to falter in the 1880s, after a boom in the 1870s. This was because of the increasing availability of cheap machine-made American and Swiss watches. The quality hand-made Coventry watch began to die out and the city's scattered watchmakers began to disappear. Some, such as Rotherham's, survived into the twentieth century by adapting production to, among other things, motor car components and fine quality machine parts. As the city held such a wealth of skilled workers, it is not surprising that the cycle industry gave birth to the British motor industry.

Possibly the forerunner of all modern cycles. The Rover Safety Cycle was designed by James Starley's nephew John Kemp Starley, of Barrs Hill House, Radford. Harry Lawson of Coventry also claimed to be the inventor of the first safety cycle

The foundation of the motor industry in Coventry can be credited to Harry J. Lawson, an engineer who claimed, like Starley, to have been the inventor of the first 'safety' cycle. Lawson saw the car was gaining momentum abroad, and decided to try to take sole control of the industry in this country. Lawson tried to corner the industry by setting up the British Motor Syndicate Ltd with Henry Sturmey and B. Van Praagh, and began to buy every patent he could lay his hands on. The most important of these were the British patent rights for the Gottlieb Daimler engine, purchased from Frederick Simms (who later became an engineering consultant for the company) for £35,000 in 1895; and also the patent rights from Léon Bollée for his motor tandem which cost £20,000.

In January 1896 Lawson formed the Daimler Motor Company, which was floated on the market. At the end of March 1896, the Daimler Company purchased a large cotton mill in Drapers Field, Radford for £8,000, and Lawson sold them a licence to build Daimler engines for £40,000. This was to become the birthplace of the British car industry; Lawson called it Motor Mills.

Meanwhile, Lawson brought Bollée over from Paris with his motor tandem and lodged him at the Queen's Hotel in Hertford Street. It was noted in *The Autocar* of 9 May 1896 that 'The venerable Mayor of Coventry (Ald. Loudon) himself became publicly engaged with the assistance of six policemen in breaking the law – in other words in riding through the streets on Mr Bollée's petroleum tricycle.' The law

A Coventry 'ordinary', as the penny farthing was called. Starley and Hillman patented the first light weight, all metal version of this cycle

was being broken because the Red Flag Act was in force: this forbade any vehicle on the open road from travelling at over 4 mph, unless preceded by a man carrying a red flag.

Bollée's vehicle was taken to the Humber factory in Lower Ford Street (as Motor Mills was not yet ready), and dismantled. Here the workers were dismayed to find that Bollée's plans for the vehicle were metric and in French, so new plans had to be made. This task was only just finished in July when Lawson received a telegram when in London; it simply read 'Works burnt down. Bollée machine and drawings lost.' Lawson caught the first train back, and while the factory ruins still smouldered, he and a group of workers searched the rubble for remains of the vehicle and drawings. Nothing remained but a few gears, nuts and bits of the car, which had plummeted through burning floors. Lawson declared, 'There's £20,000 gone up in smoke!' and wrote to Bollée asking for another machine.

The Humber works was temporarily transferred to Motor Mills. One floor of the building was occupied by E.J. Pennington, as part of a £100,000 deal for the rights of his vehicles. He was a somewhat dubious character, who made false claims for his inventions and had fled America owing money and accused of fraud.

Bollée came over to England to drive the first British-built (by Humber) Bollée out of Motor Mills, only to find that it refused to start. After a sleepless night it was suggested to Bollée that the special petrol might be at fault; benzine was tried, the engine burst into life

Motor Mills, Drapers Field, Radford: the birthplace of the British motor industry. From here in February 1897 was driven the first British-built motorcar

and the party drove to Leamington. Back in May 1896 Lawson had launched his Great Horseless Carriage Company, and in April purchased the main block of Motor Mills for £20,000 from Daimler, who kept the outside workshops, ten acres of land and a profit of £12,000. The GHCC leased two storeys of Motor Mills from Lawson and lasted for two years, despite producing no vehicles.

In November 1896 the Red Flag Act was abolished, and in January and February of 1897 the first complete British-built 4 hp Daimler-engined motor cars, a huge advance on the Bollée machine, left Motor Mills. To prove the new Daimler's reliability in April 1897, Lawson's friend and director of the Daimler Company, Henry Sturmey, drove a benzine fuelled Daimler from John o' Groats to Lands End. The 929-mile journey was completed without a hitch, and thereafter the Daimler was firmly established.

In spring 1898 the GHCC became the Motor Manufacturing Company Ltd, which produced Daimler-based cars and De-Dion-engined motorcycles and quadricycles. The MMC left Radford in 1905, moving to Parkside. Daimler took over the whole Radford works.

From these beginnings the British motor car industry was born; of the original companies only Daimler survived. Harry Lawson overreached himself and squandered thousands in his financial dealings. As English engineers were unwilling to copy foreign designs,

Harry Lawson, his wife, and Henry Sturmey (far left) at the first London to Brighton run in 1897

roadgate looking north
round 1899. This view
ad changed little until its
tal destruction in 1940

Lawson's patents became worthless, and after a number of failed patent lawsuits, Lawson was found guilty in 1904 of fraud and was sentenced to one year's hard labour. Lawson died a forgotten man in 1925, his fortune less than £10.

Nineteenth-century Coventry saw the decline of traditional trades and the emergence of modern industries. Its population reached 69,764 by 1899, because of the increase in industry, and also because of boundary extensions, adding Earlsdon, Kingfield, Radford, Red Lane in 1890, and Foleshill and Stoke in 1899. The city was prosperous and ready to meet the new century.

CHAPTER SEVENTEEN

Growth, Destruction and Resurrection

Coventry entered the twentieth century with ever growing industrial strength. Over sixty years there were seventy-three new car manufacturers and seventy-eight new motorcycle firms. By 1910 Coventry's population was over 100,000, 10,000 of whom were car-workers.

Many cycle firms adapted their factories for car production, some earlier than others. These included Triumph, Rover, Riley, Hillman and Humber. The Singer Company was established in 1874 by George Singer of Coundon Court, and first built cycles. Motorcycles followed, and the company produced its first cars in 1905. Singer was bought by the Rootes group in 1956.

During the First World War the production of luxury goods ceased in the city, and Coventry became one of the largest producers of muni-

Daimler chassis being test driven in Sandy Lane, Radford around 1908

A view from Greyfriars
Green of Coventry's
famous three spires, from
left to right, Holy Trinity,
St Michael's and
Christchurch

tions in the land. Armstrong-Whitworth, Standard and Daimler produced fighters and aero-engines. The Ordnance Works in Red Lane produced guns, shells, bullets and aeroplanes. Its workforce grew so large that the Stoke Heath estate was built to house it. The works built the first tank, but the army refused the new invention.

A huge aerodrome was built in Radford, and White and Poppe's massive munitions factory worked day and night at Whitemore Park. The bombs and bullets were stored in underground dumps until loaded into munitions trains. A total of 60,000 people were engaged in the city producing munitions, half from elsewhere. During the war 25,000 left to fight for King and Country; 2,587 did not return and they were commemorated in October 1927 with the dedication of the war memorial by Field Marshal Earl Haig, in the Memorial Park.

The end of the war was celebrated by the Godiva Peace Procession of 18 July 1919, which ended with three nights of rioting, finally stopped by police baton charges. This may have taken place because of rumours that some shops in Broadgate were German-owned, or perhaps because Lady Godiva rode fully clothed!

During the previous year St Michael's church had become a cathedral. The new bishop was Hugh Yeatmann-Biggs, whose tomb can still be seen in the ruins of St Michael's.

Royal visits during this period include that of George V in 1915; Queen Mary in 1917; the Duke of York (later George VI), who officially opened the Council House in 1920; and Edward, Prince of Wales in 1923.

In 1928 the city boundaries were extended again, taking in parts of Foleshill, Stoke Heath, Stoke, Whitley, Cheylesmore, Canley, Tile Hill, Westwood Heath, Eastern Green, Allesley and Stoneleigh. In 1932 Wyken, Walsgrave, Binley, Willenhall, Styvechale, Coundon and part of Keresley and Exhall were added.

As traffic increased city officials decided to open up the city's medieval streets. What was called 'slum clearance' began at the start of the century, and in the subsequent road schemes Coventry lost many of its finest pre-seventeenth-century buildings. In 1929 work began to build Corporation Street (opened in 1931), which resulted in a massive swathe of land being cleared – far greater than was needed for the project. Ancient timber buildings and Victorian brick alike were brought crashing to the ground. The Prince of Wales saw plans for the latest 'clearance' during his visit in 1934. This slum was one of the city's finest medieval streets, known as Butcher Row. From the beginning of 1936 hundreds of pre-eighteenth-century buildings were destroyed in Butcher Row, Bull Ring, Trinity Lane, Little Butcher Row, Cross Cheaping, Ironmonger Row, Palmer Lane and beyond

Although this illustration dates from the mid-nineteenth century this view of Butcher Row remained largely unchanged until its demolition in 1936

The cathedral church of St Michael the day after its destruction by incendiaries. Many of the cathedral's treasures were destroyed when the roof collapsed into the blazing interior

Broadgate is laid waste in this view looking towards Holy Trinity

New Buildings. The result of this vandalism was Trinity Street (opened in 1937), the brainchild of Alderman Wyles in 1910.

It was not to end here, for soon the world was once again at war. Coventry's factories once more began the production of war weapons, and Whitley and Lancaster bombers were produced at the Armstrong-Whitworth plant at Whitley. The Rootes Group produced bombers and military vehicles, Standard produced Gypsy Moths and Mosquitoes and Jaguar made bomber and fighter parts and military vehicles. Daimler produced 50,000 aero-engines, armoured and scout cars and Alvis produced armoured vehicles and tanks. This mass production made Coventry an obvious target for the Luftwaffe.

One of the most devastating dates in Coventry's history was 14 November 1940. On that day news came that a heavy raid was to take place, probably in London. Churchill rushed back to the capital, not wishing to be out of London on such a night. He stood watching on the roof of a government building, but nothing happened. Meanwhile Bomber Command was tracking German bombers heading north, and soon the command centre under Coventry's main post office building in Hertford Street began to track aircraft heading for Coventry. The night was cloudless, with a clear hunter's moon reflecting on the rooftops. Just before 7 o'clock a distant drone could be heard, growing louder and louder. The sirens wailed.

At 7.20 p.m. incendiaries rained down, landing on St Michael's, Palace Yard, Broadgate and Owen Owen. The city centre was ablaze.

99

By 7.30 high explosives began falling from the stream of bombers that droned overhead. Searchlights scanned the sky as ack-ack blasted the heavens. The devastation continued as Coventry burnt, amid massive explosions which tore the city apart. The Revd Richard Howard, Jack Forbes, Mr Eaton and Mr White, on the roof of St Michael's, supplied only with stirrup pumps and sand, fought against falling incendiaries, until fire took hold in the roof space. As the roof blazed and beams began to fall, they rushed into the cathedral to save all they could. Eventually the fire brigade arrived, only to find the water main smashed. They had to stand back to watch the great cathedral burn.

For eleven long hours over 500 bombers unloaded 500 tons of high explosives and 30,000 incendiaries on the city's heart. At about 6.15 a.m. the onslaught ended. The human cost of that night was 554 dead and 865 injured, with 45,000 homes and 75 per cent of Coventry's industry lost or severely damaged.

Overnight destruction on this scale had never been witnessed before, and the Germans coined a new word for it, 'Coventrated'. The bombing raid left the city without the most basic services. Coventry's trams, would never run again, as the system was totally wiped out. On 16 November George VI arrived in the city to see the destruction. As troops began to help clear up and uncover the dead, 'Business as usual' signs began to appear among the ruins.

On 8 April 1941 another devastating raid raised the death toll to 1,200 with 1,746 injured.

Amid the rubble the rebuilding of the city centre got under way, and in May 1948 Princess Elizabeth opened the new enlarged island Broadgate. The following year the statue of Godiva was unveiled. Several buildings which survived the blitz, including the market clock tower, were demolished to clear the way for a pedestrian precinct, envisaged by city architect Donald Gibson. The building began with the construction of Broadgate House, opened in May 1953. This was followed by Woolworth's, Marks and Spencer and British Home Stores. In 1955 the Upper Precinct was completed. Gibson left the city in 1955, and the work was continued by Arthur Ling who extended the road begun by Gibson through the pedestrian area into Market Way, thus enlarging the precinct. The work was finally finished by Terence Gregory.

Plans for the replacement of Coventry Cathedral received urgent attention. Sir Gilbert Scott's design was dropped after a competition, won by Basil Spence. He envisaged a new cathedral built on the burial ground of the old. John Laing and Co. began work in 1955, and the queen laid the foundation stone in March 1956. The project received

he old and the new.
etween Holy Trinity and
e old cathedral rises the
ew cathedral of St
lichael. The new church
aught the imagination of
e world's press and is
elieved by many to be
ae of the greatest
aildings of the period

world-wide attention and funds, and the building was completed on 26 April 1962, when the 90-ft bronze flèche was placed on the roof.

The '50s and '60s were a boom period for Coventry; with massive car production and ownership, it earned the nickname 'Car City'. Industry brought immigration, swelling the population to over 300,000 in the 1960s, with over 60,000 working in the motor industry. Other industries were machine-tool makers, aircraft-engines, military vehicles, electrical components, telecommunications, the nylon and Rayon industry and rubber based industries.

In 1960 Jaguar took control of Daimler, and British Leyland bought out Standard-Triumph. In 1966 Jaguar itself became part of the British Motor Corporation, along with Triumph, Daimler, Rover, Standard and Alvis. Chrysler bought out Rootes in the same year, and in 1979

The Upper Precinct today

Chrysler itself was bought by Peugeot-Citroen. The company was renamed Talbot, and later became Peugeot-Talbot.

During the late 1970s until the present, economic recessions have bitten deeply into the city's industrial base, and many large firms have closed. The car industry has declined greatly, leaving only Jaguar-Daimler and Peugeot-Talbot.

Coventry itself is changing, becoming a more commercial city: most of its new buildings are offices and shops rather than factories. Commercial expansion has taken place at Westwood Heath and at the Walsgrave Triangle. Some London-based firms have relocated here.

For the first time since the completion of Broadgate and the Precinct, modern development has taken place in the main shopping area. Cathedral Lanes opened in November 1990, built on part of the original Broadgate and the site of Coventry Gaol. This was followed in April 1991 with the opening of West Orchard shopping centre.

Coventry's redevelopment was achieved at a cost. After the Second World War, despite enemy bombing, over 350 buildings dating from before the seventeenth century survived. These survivors were whittled down to a mere thirty-four by 1966. The trend was not halted, but whatever the future holds for Coventry, it can remain proud of its historic past.

A Tour of Central Coventry

Start in the old cathedral.

St Michael's was built mainly during the fourteenth and fifteenth centuries. The original church, which existed in 1138, probably stood in the area of the south porch. Until it became a cathedral in 1918 this was the largest parish church in England. The tower and spire, once said to 'rank with the wonders of the world,' were built by the merchant Botoner family, begun in the fourteenth century, and are the third tallest in England, measuring nearly 300 ft.

The old cathedral of St Michael as it looked in 1940 before its destruction

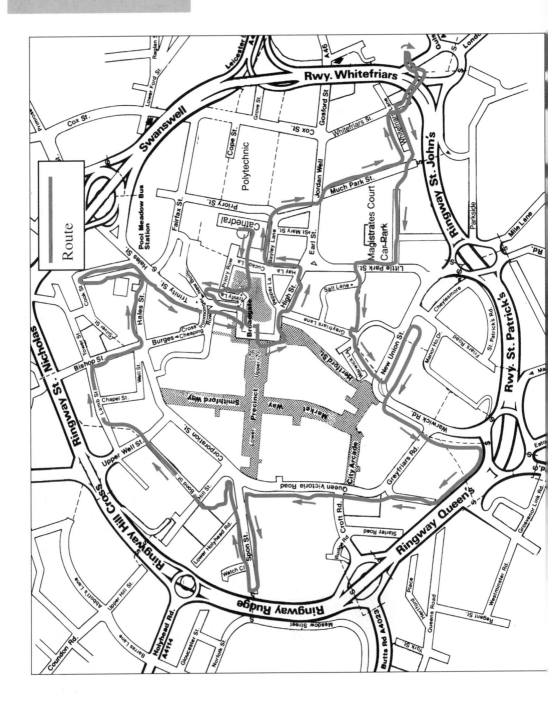

St Michael's was the only English cathedral to be destroyed in the Second World War (chapter seventeen). Few of its treasures survived the destruction, and the magnificent church was left a mere shell. The morning after its destruction, Jack Forbes, the church mason, took two charred roof timbers from the smouldering rubble and bound them together to form a cross, which he planted among the ruins. He also built an altar on which was placed the cross and a cross of nails. Behind this were carved the words 'Father Forgive'.

Cross into the new cathedral.

Sir Basil Spence, designer of the new cathedral said: 'The author of this design does not see this building as a planning problem, but the opportunity to create a Shrine to the Glory of God.' Unique in many aspects, the sheer walls were inspired by Norman architecture. Building began in 1955 and was completed in 1962. Many of the period's finest artists worked on its interior. The west screen, designed by John Hutton and engraved with angels and saints, gives a view straight into the building. Beyond it can be seen Graham Sutherland's

The new cathedral of St Michael, one of the greatest buildings of the post-war era and a centre of world reconciliation

tapestry, 'Christ in Glory', originally the largest in the world. Stained glass is by John Piper and the 25-ft statue of St Michael defeating the devil by the steps was the last major work of Jacob Epstein.

The Visitors' Centre holds treasures from the old and new cathedrals, and audio-visual displays explain their history.

A ghostly monk once haunted this site.

> **Walk up St Michael's Avenue to the gravestone on the right.**

Here lies John Parkes, 'The Invincible', one of Europe's greatest eighteenth-century gladiators, who fought 350 bloody combats. Georgian gladiators fought on raised circular stages, for money and honour. Parkes was an expert with the razor-tipped, two-handed sword, which was $3^1/_2$ ft long. With shaven head, white jacket, breeches and stockings and a ribbon on the sword arm, gladiators fought until they were totally outclassed or severely wounded. A huge facial wound or loss of an ear was not considered the end, as gladiators were used to being stitched up at ringside while sipping wine.

As a swordsman Parkes was described as slow, cunning, precise and lethal. His skills included the use of the sword and dagger and, as one poster for a London fight shows, flails. This man of 'mild disposition' certainly earned his place in Coventry's history.

> **Walk up to the Cross.**

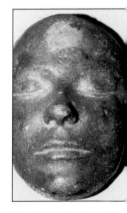

This smaller copy of Coventry Cross was erected in 1976, a gift to the city from the Coventry Boys Foundation (chapter eleven). To the left of the cross is the site where Mary Ball of Nuneaton was hanged in 1846, for poisoning her husband with arsenic. The gallows were draped with black crepe and as the bell of St Michael's struck eleven, Mary was led out to the gallows. Her hand was bandaged, for the prison chaplain, who was later dismissed, had held it over a candle to show her how she would burn if she didn't repent.

Over 30,000 people witnessed this last public execution, after which Mary Ball was taken back into the gaol. Here her death-mask was made before her body was buried 16 ft below the gaol yard, where she probably still remains. Coventry Gaol, a large institution with its own treadmill, stood on this site from at least the seventeenth century until July 1860, when the last prisoner was transferred to Warwick. The

The plaster death mask of Mary Ball taken after she was hanged. It is now located in the Black Museum, Police Headquarters, Little Park Street

County Hall, built in 1785 and once attached to the gaol, lost its status in 1842, when the County of the City of Coventry was abolished.

Walk down the lane and into Trinity church.

The first church here was built by the monks of St Mary's Priory sometime after 1043. The present building dates from the early thirteenth and late fifteenth centuries, with the exception of the spire. This was built in 1667 to replace one which had collapsed, killing a boy. The church once contained a series of chapels, and still has a splendid painted medieval roof and Doom painting: there is also a fifteenth-century pulpit, the highest in England, by which stand a brass eagle lectern and painted font of the same date.

In the Archdeacon's Court, where ecclesiastical matters were once dealt with, are various monuments, including that of Dr Philemon Holland. England's greatest eighteenth-century actress, Sarah Siddons, was married here in November 1773, and Mary Ann Evans (George Eliot) attended this church with her father, who was plate-bearer.

Leave church, turn right to cottages, look over the railings.

This was the west entrance to St Mary's priory church, dedicated October 1043 and once one of the greatest monastic houses and places of pilgrimage in England. The cathedral stretched from here as far as the new cathedral, where remains of its east end can be seen. Many monarchs have stayed here, the last to walk through this entrance being Henry VIII, who was responsible for the building's destruction. Below this hillside lie crypts and mysterious tunnels, and the tombs of Lady Godiva and Earl Leofric.

The cottages, once called Lych Gate House, were built by the Revd John Bryan, vicar of Holy Trinity from 1644 to 1662.

Into Trinity Street and turn right.

This is the largest remaining piece of the priory church above ground – part of a tower base, which made up the west entrance. An identical tower stood on the site of Bryan's cottage. In the street note the building with the large windows, the only surviving weaving factory in the city centre. Here steam-driven silk looms were first introduced by Beck, whose factory was burnt down by a mob (chapter sixteen). New Buildings was created during the Civil War (1642–5) to accommodate people whose homes outside the city walls were demolished.

Go up Trinity Street to Broadgate.

Broadgate has been the heart of the city for over 1,000 years. First mentioned by name in the twelfth century, the 'Broad-yate' served as the main entrance to Coventry Castle. Kings and queens have passed through and been entertained here, armies have walked here and barbaric executions have taken place. Broadgate was widened in 1820, and most of its medieval buildings were demolished. Old Broadgate was completely destroyed on 14 November 1940, and a new island Broadgate was opened in May 1948 as the first stage of the centre's redevelopment.

The Godiva statue, sculpted in bronze by Sir William Reid Dick, was presented to the city by William Bassett Green, a descendant of Eli Green, a Coventry ribbon weaver manufacturer. The statue was unveiled in October 1949 and was moved a few yards on the completion of Cathedral Lanes. The Godiva puppet clock at the top of Broadgate was made by sculptor Trevor Tennant, and is powered by a mechanism made by Coventry clockmaker Edward Loseby in 1870 and used in the old market hall clock.

Cross into Upper Precinct.

The Upper Precinct was the first pedestrian precinct in the world. Basically following the line of old Smithford Street, it was built in the 1950s. The 'levelling stone' carved with Coventry's phoenix, symbolizing resurrection, was unveiled in 1948. To the left of the stone was the birthplace of Dame Ellen Terry in Market Street (destroyed 1940). Dame Ellen became one of England's greatest Victorian actresses.

Return to Broadgate, turn half right, and walk along High Street.

The National Westminster Bank, built in 1930–1, is the only prewar building to survive in Broadgate. Greyfriars Lane was the original thoroughfare into Broadgate before Hertford Street was built in 1813. Further down High Street on the right is one of the city's few surviving old inns. The Rose and Crown (recently renamed The Courtyard) was said to have accommodated the notorious highwayman Dick Turpin for one night, as he travelled to York.

Continue along High Street, and turn left into Hay Lane.

The Council House was built between 1913 and 1917, and was officially opened by George VI in 1920. The building is interesting for the carvings that adorn it. The Portland Stone figures around the entrance showing Leofric, Godiva and others associated with the city's history, were added in 1925.

Walk down Hay Lane.

Hay Lane has the typical narrowness of a medieval street. The buildings on the right, some of which date from the seventeenth century, have recently been restored. Down this cobbled lane criminals were brought in carts, sitting upon their own coffins, on their way to the gallows. The Golden Cross is traditionally the site of the Coventry Mint, which struck gold and silver coins between 1466 and 1470 (chapter nine). The seventeenth-century inn was restored in the nineteenth century, using timbers from the old bell-frame of St Michael's.

Turn right into Bayley Lane.

No. 22 Bayley Lane is a fine sixteenth-century half-timbered building of a type once common in the city. Note the carved corner post and barge boards, another once typical feature on Coventry buildings.

Walk through the gates into Castle Yard.

Castle Yard opened in 1992 as part of the completion of a building programme and restoration scheme. This is part of the site of Coventry Castle, a building with a short and violent history. The buildings on the right once formed part of the White Horse Inn, to which this entrance led. The building on the left is St Mary's Hall, and the stone tower at the rear is Caesar's Tower, possibly part of the castle. It was destroyed in the Second World War and rebuilt. Here Mary Queen of Scots was imprisoned by order of Elizabeth I (see chapter eleven).

Leave yard and continue along Bayley Lane.

St Mary's Guildhall was built in the late fourteenth and early fifteenth centuries as a base for the city's powerful guilds. Note the carvings in the vaulted entrance; you are now walking in the footsteps of many monarchs, such as Henry VI, Henry VII and James I, and novelists such as Charles Dickens and George Eliot. Here Godiva has mounted her horse since 1678, using 'Godiva's mounting block', a cylindrical stone.

Inside are many treasures, including a huge fifteenth-century tapestry showing the marriage of Henry VII. It was a place of civic occasion for centuries, and has a medieval decorated truss roof; paintings of English monarchs adorn the walls and can also be found in the stained glass. There is a minstrels' gallery bearing the remains of the city's once huge armoury; all of this armour saw service. This is one of the finest guildhalls in the land.

Continue to the bottom of Bayley Lane.

An engraving by Taunton showing Bayley Lane in 1850. Little has changed here for 500 years except for the loss of a number of timber-framed buildings

The Drapers' Hall was built by the city drapers for meetings and social events, and opened in November 1832. Many grand balls were held here in the past.

Cross to the opposite corner.

Below what is now the Tourist Information Centre is a perfect fourteenth-century cellar, one of the few which still survive in the city. Next door can be found the city record office and the museum which has displays of local history, natural history and art.

Follow the lane to the right and cross into Much Park Street.

The Stone House, a medieval merchant's house, dating from around 1350, is on the left. It survived because like many of the city's timber

Whitefriars Gate for many years served as cottages. One of its inhabitants in the eighteenth century was called Mother Shipton, and was known locally as a wise woman who, like her earlier northern counterpart, predicted future events and cast spells

buildings it was sandwiched in bricks. During the blitz the outer shell was blown off, revealing this ancient gem. In past centuries many important citizens lived along this road, which joined the London Road. Michael Drayton served here as page to Sir Henry Goodere.

Continue to the stone gateway.

This is Whitefriars Gate, which was built in 1352 and formed the outer gateway to Whitefriars Monastery. Charles Dickens describes it in *The Old Curiosity Shop*: the image apparently stuck in his mind after he passed the gate one moonlit night in a stagecoach. It now contains a toy museum.

Go through the gate and follow signs for Whitefriars.

Whitefriars Monastery once boasted a spired church and outbuildings. Founded by Sir John Poultney in 1342, the cloistered building survived the Dissolution, as it was converted into a private house by John Hales. Elizabeth I and James I both stayed here. The building was converted into a workhouse in 1801, and in 1943 it became a hostel. It is now a museum and art gallery.

Return by the same route, and cut through from Much Park Street via footpath on left of the street to Little Park Street. Cross over.

Kirby House has a handsome Georgian façade, which dates from the 1730s. This façade, however, is only skin-deep for behind it is a new building, rebuilt using some of the original material. Martyrs were led down Little Park Street to the stake at Park Hollows. A memorial to them stands at the end of the street.

Turn right and walk along Little Park Street. Turn left into Salt Lane, on the left, and follow footpath into Greyfriars Lane.

Ford's Hospital was founded by William Ford in 1509 to provide shelter for five aged men and one woman, and is one of the finest domestic buildings in England. In 1517 William Pisford left money so

Kirby House was named after solicitor Thomas Kirby, whose office was here in the 1870s. The original building was far older with an interior dating from the seventeenth century

A mid-Victorian engraving of Ford's Hospital, unchanged to this day. Buildings of such quality were once a common sight in Coventry

that more inmates could be taken within its walls, and by the eighteenth century the institution had become exclusively female. A direct hit from a single bomb, just after midnight on 14 October 1940, killed the warden, a nurse and six inmates. The almshouse was restored in 1953 using material from the rear, which was beyond repair. During restoration it was discovered that the building was made mainly of teak, a great rarity.

Turn back towards road junction (and spire), and follow footpath (half right) to New Union Street.

113

Christchurch spire is the third of Coventry's three famous spires. The church was originally part of a Franciscan monastery, built here in the fourteenth century. The monastery, together with the main body of the church, was demolished during the Dissolution in 1539. The spire stood alone in an orchard, and was at one point used as a pigsty. The body of the church was rebuilt in 1830–1, and was changed from Greyfriars to Christchurch. The church was once

A mid-nineteenth century view of Christchurch, showing its second nave, which was destroyed during the war. When the ancient ball and weather-vane were regilded in 1831 the ball was found to have been hit a number of times by musket shot

again destroyed during the raid of April 1941, and the spire stood alone once more.

Cross the road.

No. 1 The Quadrant was the home from 1911 of Angela Brazil, one of England's best-known writers of schoolgirl novels. She died in 1947.

Walk up New Union Street to Cannon Bollards, and turn right.

Cheylesmore Gatehouse, now the registry office, was the sixteenth-century gatehouse to Cheylesmore Manor House. The manor, built in the thirteenth century, once belonged to the Black Prince, who enjoyed hunting here so tradition says. The royal residence was in a ruinous state by the seventeenth century. Later converted into cottages it was finally demolished in 1956, leaving the gatehouse standing alone.

Return through The Quadrant to Warwick Road. Cross over and turn left.

The statue here is of Sir Thomas White, London merchant and benefactor. In 1542 he gave £1,400 to purchase land to be held in trust

Through this gateway on the left, in the sixteenth century, stood medieval Cheylesmore Manor House. The building was long, and had a sandstone base and timber-framed walls. Cutting across the end of the building was the city wall

115

for charitable purposes in Coventry. The income from these lands, now £40,000 a year, is distributed to deserving causes. The statue was erected in 1882.

Continue along Warwick Row.

The last building in Warwick Row was the private school of the Franklin sisters. Here from 1832–5, Mary Ann Evans (George Eliot) was educated. Mary Ann based her deportment and voice on Rebecca Franklin, her teacher, who aspired to 'Parisian' manners gained during her time on the continent.

Next to the building can be seen the Starley Memorial, erected in honour of James Starley, 'Father of the Cycle Industry' (see chapter sixteen).

Turn right on to the Ringway, turn next right, left into Queen Victoria Road, and left into Spon Street.

In Spon Street there are many rebuilt fifteenth- to seventeenth-century buildings from other parts of the city, as well as some of the street's original buildings. This gives some idea of how the city may once have looked. The original Windmill Inn retains much of its old-

The entrance to Spon Street was one of the places where the Coventry mystery plays were enacted.

Mid-nineteenth-century engraving of St John's church. The area around here, once the site of the Babba-lake, was up until early this century prone to flooding. In December 1900 the interior of the church was flooded up to a depth of 4 ft

world charm. At the entrance to the street can be seen two pieces of sandstone wall, placed above the line of the original city wall, which joined Spon Gate at this point. A piece of the original wall can be seen in the wall of the building opposite.

Continue to the bottom of Spon Street, where St John's church, Fleet Street, can be seen.

The church of St John the Baptist was founded by Queen Isabella in May 1344, so that priests would pray here for her family, England and the soul of Edward II. It fell from use after 1539, and after the battle of Preston, in 1648, prisoners were held here. The church was also used as stables, a market and a winding and dyeing house, finally becoming a parish church in 1734.

Go through the gate next to the church, and turn right.

On the left is Bond's Hospital, founded by Thomas Bond for poor aged men in 1506. In 1619 one, Johnstone, poisoned eight of the almshouse's inmates, and then poisoned himself. He was buried at midnight before a huge crowd at the roadside outside Cook Street Gate.

Across the quadrangle is Bablake School, founded by Thomas Wheatley (later mayor) in 1560, for the education of boys. The school was founded following an amazing windfall. When Wheatley ordered a chest of steel ingots from Spain, he received a chest of silver ingots. As he could not trace the source he used the silver to found the school.

Cross Hill Street, and follow Bond Street along the line of the city wall; cross into Upper Well Street passage.

This constitutes the only remains of a round tower, one of many which once dotted the city wall. Originally much higher, it probably once housed a cannon and stores.

Turn right into Lamb Street, right again into Bishop Street, and cross over.

The Old Grammar School was originally the church of the Hospital of St John. This hospital was built in the twelfth century to provide refuge for the sick, poor and wayfarers in need. The church, built in the fourteenth century, was converted into a grammar school by John Hales of Whitefriars in the sixteenth century, and remained a school until 1885. Elizabeth I inspected the school's library and presented money for its upkeep on her visit in 1565. The building originally extended across what is now Hales Street.

Turn left into Hales Street.

Coventry Transport Museum holds the largest display of British-made cars, motorcycles and bicycles in the world. It covers the history of road transport, and various motor-related events are held there.

Turn left into St Agnes Lane.

Cook Street Gate is one of the two surviving city gates from the original twelve. At the side can be seen the doorways which led on to the wall, and marked on the gate is the distance to Leicester in miles marked in Roman numerals. During the 1404 parliament in Coventry,

Swanswell Gate. The lower room is formed from the original archway and the upper room led on to the city wall

the prior complained that rubbish dumped near this gate obstructed his carriage. The gate was given to the city by Col. Sir William Wyley in 1913, and was restored in 1918 and 1931.

Between Cook Street Gate and Swanswell Gate lies a complete stretch of the city wall, although only half its original thickness and not as high. This area was converted into a memorial garden and presented to the city in 1932 by Sir Alfred Herbert, industrialist. His wife's initials can be seen on the surrounding bronze railing.

Walk through the garden.

Swanswell or Priory Gate was built by request of the Prior of Coventry in 1461. It was later converted into a cottage, and became a shop in the nineteenth century. The gate was restored in 1931–2 and was presented to the city by Sir Alfred Herbert. Up White Street lies Swanswell Pool, once known as 'Swineswell'. Legend says that it was formed by a giant wild boar which terrorized the area until dispatched by Sir Guy of Warwick. The huge blade-bone claimed to belong either to the boar or a monstrous Dun Cow also killed by Sir Guy, which hung on the outside of St George's chapel, was thrown into the Swanswell in the 1850s.

Return to Broadgate via Hales St and Trinity Street.

Acknowledgements

Many thanks to Neil Cowley (drawings) and Barry Denton of the Sealed Knot; West Midlands Police, Little Park St; and C.M. Barlow for photographs; Graham Lindsay for engravings and photos from family scrapbooks; and Frank Vince for engravings from the *Gentleman's Magazine* and other illustrations. Also thanks to the City Engineer's Transportation Section for use of the central area map.

Many thanks to Heather Head for help with typing and proof-reading and Coventry Local Studies Library for their useful assistance.

Bibliography

Andrews Cuttings, Coventry Warwickshire collection, Central Library

Anglo-Saxon Chronicle, translated by G.N. Garmonsway, Dent, 1972

Burbidge, F.B., *Old Coventry and Lady Godiva*, Birmingham, 1952

Cassells Illustrated History of England, c. 1850

Coventry Evening Telegraph

Coventry Herald, 1800–50, Coventry Warwickshire collection

Coventry Mercury 1745–1830, Coventry Warwickshire collection

Coventry Standard 1900–1950, Coventry Warwickshire collection

Dibben, A.A., *Coventry City Charters*, Coventry Papers, 1969

Fox, L., *Coventry's Heritage, Coventry Evening Telegraph*, 1947

Gentleman's Magazine, 1790–1820, private collection

Gooder, E., *Coventry's Town Wall*, Coventry and Warwickshire history pamphlet, 1971

Harris, M.D., *The Coventry Leet Book*, Early English Text Society, 1907–13

Harris M.D., *The Story of Coventry*, London, 1911

Hobley, B., *Excavations of St Mary's, Coventry*, Birmingham and Warwickshire Archaeological Society, 1971

Hole, C., *English Folk Heroes*, Batsford, 1948

Hole, C., *Witchcraft in England*, Batsford, 1971

Lancaster, J., *Official Guide to St Mary's Hall*, Coventry Corporation, 1948

Long, J., *Marques of Coventry*, Warwickshire Books, 1990

Macfarlane. C. and Thomson, Revd T., *Comprehensive History of England*, 1860

McGrory, D., *Around Coventry in Old Photographs*, Alan Sutton, 1991

Masterman, Revd J., *Coventry and its Story*, Coventry Education Committee, *c.* 1910

Midland Daily Telegraph, 1900–1950, Coventry Warwickshire collection

Mowat, R.B., *A New History of Great Britain*, Oxford University Press, 1920

Newdigate, B., *Michael Drayton and his Circle,* Oxford, 1941

Phythian-Adams, C., *Desolation of a City*, Cambridge University Press, 1979

Pollard, A., *English Miracle Plays*, Oxford, 1923

Poole, B., *Coventry: its History and Antiquities*, Coventry, 1870

Reader, W., manuscripts edited by C. Nowell, Coventry Warwickshire collection

Rylatt, M. and Gooder, E., *City of Coventry: Archaeology and Development*, Coventry Museums, 1977

Shelton, J.B., *Austin Monthly* (magazine), 1932–6

Smith, F., *Coventry: Six Hundred Years of Municipal Life*, Coventry Corporation, 1945

Victoria County History, Vol. VIII, London, 1969

Ward, A.C., *Illustrated History of English Literature*, Longman, 1953

Woodhouse, F.W., *Churches of Coventry*, London, 1909

ADDRESSES

Local Studies Section. Central Library, Smithford Way. (0203) 25555.
City Record Office. Bayley Lane. 25555. ext. 2768.
Herbert Art Gallery and Museum. Jordan Well. 832381
Museum of British Road Transport. Hales Street. 832425.
Coventry Black Museum. West Midlands Police, Little Park Street. 555333
Lunt Roman Fort. Baginton. 832433
Whitefriars. London Road. 832433
Midland Air Museum. Baginton. 301033.

Index